MARKETPLACE
MISSIONAL

Finding Your
Everyday Work in
God's Eternal Plan

ERIK COOPER

WHAT PEOPLE ARE SAYING

In *Missional Marketplace*, Erik Cooper speaks with rare clarity and understanding of the marketplace as a place of mission. As a master storyteller, he takes the reader into the streets of the town square and shows how a daily trip to work is a journey along the road of God's purpose. The insights of these pages have the power and potential to reshape how you view work and see God's fingerprints at each turn of the road that has led you to your marketplace calling. Get ready to see new life in your story!

- Michael Messner
CEO, Assemblies of God Business as Mission

What I love about Erik Cooper is that he makes much of Jesus and is little in his own eyes. What I love about his book is that it makes much of Jesus and has large implications for God's work in God's world. The greatest way to fulfill the Great Commandment is in full-hearted pursuit of the Great Commission. Erik's wit and wisdom leads us into the Great Story and reveals that our work is of eternal value, whatever it is and wherever it is done, when it spreads God's global glory among all nations.

- Dick Brogden
Co-Founder of the Live Dead Movement

Erik Cooper addresses the perceived dichotomy between secular and sacred calling. It is a courageous endeavor. There is no doubt that each believer is called to Kingdom work in the harvest fields of the world. The key is discerning God's specific call and yielding to His placement.

- Dr. Greg Mundis
Executive Director, Assemblies of God World Missions

For over twenty-five years I have served in the intersection of work, business, and ministry. I have interviewed hundreds of Christian entrepreneurs, read dozens of books on the topic, and attended numerous workshops and seminars that focused on helping people understand how to live out their calling and mission through their work. Based on my firsthand experience, I can say that there are very few individuals who are better suited and equipped to write on this topic than Erik Cooper, a true subject matter expert who has dedicated his life to this very important cause. If you are serious about understanding what God and His Word have to say about serving Jesus through work and business, then this book will give you a comprehensive and accurate framework for discovering and living out your marketplace calling.

- Ray Hilbert
Co-Founder, Truth At Work, and Founder, Kingdom-Factor

Missional Marketplace brings clarity around a question that you, or others around you, are earnestly asking: Where does my work life fit into God's grand, unfolding Kingdom story? Erik Cooper's book is relevant to any marketplace believer—from new graduates to experienced professionals decades into their careers. Dive into the theology of work and gain a fresh perspective and renewed purpose for your calling.

- Rob Hoskins
President, OneHope, Inc.

I love people who think differently about business, entrepreneurship, and the role the marketplace plays in the Great Commission. In *Missional Marketplace*, Erik unpacks how to think differently and use your role to expand God's kingdom. For over thirty years he and his family have built a Kingdom business, donating half their profits to world missions. That is living on mission! I believe this book will inspire you to use your marketplace gifts in new ways for the glory of God.

- Rob Ketterling
Lead Pastor, River Valley Church

I've really enjoyed getting to know Erik Cooper and his dad over the past few years. The way The Stone Table strategically leverages its role in the business world to partner with the local church and multiply its global missions impact is a model for the future. I pray that their story and this book inspire countless more followers of Jesus to fully engage the marketplace as a Kingdom calling.

- Rod Loy
Lead Pastor, First Assembly of God North Little Rock

Erik Cooper addresses the one thing that occupies the bulk of our time and concentration: work. Employing skillful prose and engaging images, Erik defines work's origins and meaning in God's creation and redemption of our world. And once you see it, you can't stop seeing it. God, redeeming everything in Christ for His glory—including, and especially, our work.

- Dr. Rob Shipley
Area Director Russia and Belarus, Assemblies of God World Missions

Erik Cooper doesn't just talk about faith, work, and global missions—he lives them out! I've seen him do it and I'm in awe of his heart and mind focused on God's plan. If you are a Christian in the marketplace, this is a must-read!

- Susan Rozzi
President of Rozzi and Associates

For years, we've not focused enough on helping people understand the theology of their everyday work. This book will help change that. I have heard Erik speak passionately about the principles in this book at our church as a guest speaker, traveling around the world on missions trips, and just sharing meals together. The words of this book are incarnated in Erik's life, his conversations, and his family.

- Wayne Murray
Lead Pastor, Grace Assembly of God

Erik's book is a deep dive into the paradigm shift that is necessary for today's church to be who we need to be. Overall, Erik's unique history as both a vocational minister and businessman makes all the difference in this book and in his mentorship of my business and ministry.

- BAM practitioner in creative access nation

In *Missional Marketplace*, Erik Cooper takes us through the powerful process of the gospel. By illuminating God's original intent for each person's vocation, Cooper creates a space in our hearts for the Holy Spirit to work. Once personally transformed, we are challenged to become part of God's great plan to redeem the world. Cooper leaves us feeling both encouraged and empowered to be all that God created us to be. Let's get to work!

- Adam Detamore
Lead Pastor, Realife Church

To my dad, Dave Cooper

You gave the last thirty years of your career to build something you didn't own, but you never thought of it that way. You never complained or even considered it a sacrifice. You just put your head down and went to work every day using your God-given business gifts to create something beautiful. You were business as mission before it was cool.

You always dreamed of having a million dollars. You've made that million countless times over, Dad. It may not be in a retirement account bearing interest for you and Mom, but it's in the lives of countless people all over the world bearing fruit for God's kingdom.

I'm so proud to be your son. You've given us the greatest inheritance a family could ask for: a Kingdom legacy. You gave your story over to God's Great Story. And look what God has done.

You're the richest man I know, Dad, hands down.

I love you,

Erik

TABLE OF CONTENTS

PREFACE

I can't recall hearing one sermon about work until my late 30s. My church talked a lot about money, and rightfully so. How we spend, invest, and give money as followers of Jesus is a reflection of the gospel's redemptive work in our lives. I remember a lot of messages about tithes and offerings, about giving God the "firstfruits" of our income, and about the blessings of sacrificial giving. I'm grateful for these foundational messages. They continue to shape the way I think about the resources I've been blessed with to this day. But while I encountered countless teachings about how to handle the earnings from my work, I never heard anyone speak about the underlying role of the work itself. I certainly never heard the marketplace characterized as a sacred endeavor or calling. This lack of clarity allowed my imagination to fill in the blanks. I assumed the marketplace was where sincere Christians (who had no real discernable calling) bravely infiltrated the secular sphere to drag back heathen assets for the true Kingdom heroes to utilize in the real sacred endeavors.

As my own employment journey moved me back and forth from the marketplace to full-time ministry and back again, I could sense something deeply gospel-centric about both arenas. Through a season of spiritual research and exploration, I was slowly introduced to a rich theology of work already present in some historic Christian circles. This theology of work wasn't anything new. In fact, it was something very, very old—like Genesis 1 old. I felt like I had discovered a treasure that had been buried beneath the foundation of my house for decades that I had no knowledge of. It inspired such an awakening in me that I had to share it with others, and I loved seeing the excitement and joy this integration of faith and work stirred in the hearts of my Christian friends who worked in the marketplace as well.

The first time I ever spoke about faith and work at a local church, a line of people formed down front after I dismissed the service. It was still somewhat of a new topic to me, so my gut reaction was a semi-insecure "oh boy, what heresy did I accidentally swerve into today?" Since none of them appeared to be brandishing pitchforks, I cautiously engaged. As I approached the group, I noticed tears in the eyes of one man. His shaky words still resonate in my soul: "I've worked in the business world for thirty years, and this is the first time I ever felt like the work I do each day actually matters to God." I've heard that response multiple times now over the past few years. From entrepreneurs to assembly line workers, from high-paid execs to minimum-wage hospitality staff, more Christians are becoming overwhelmingly filled with renewed purpose as they realize that the work they give over half of their waking hours to over the course of forty to fifty years on this earth has a role in God's kingdom plan.

Is there any eternal value to my day job?

Is it possible to find gospel meaning in my "secular" career?

If I really love Jesus, shouldn't I quit my job and go into full-time ministry?

How does my everyday work have anything to do with God's mission in the world?

Many marketplace Christians have wrestled with these questions in some form or fashion at some point in their lives and in their work. But even as a lifelong believer, *and* the grandson of a pastor and the son of a Christian entrepreneur, it's not a conversation I grew up having in my family or at my church.

Recently, I had the opportunity to speak at another local Indianapolis church on the sacredness of the marketplace. As the pastor, a dear personal friend, introduced me to his sizable congregation, he confessed: "I've been your pastor for twenty years, and it never even occurred to me to talk about where you spend half your waking hours each day." I'm glad to see and hear the conversation changing. Shining a light on the marketplace *and* its role in the mission of God in the world is part of our calling at The Stone Table.

Before he passed away, Billy Graham said: "I believe that one of the next great moves of God is going to be through the believers in the workplace."[1] The gospel is waiting to resurrect our everyday work and transform it into what God always intended it to be: a tangible way to both *demonstrate and proclaim* the kingdom of God and the lordship of Christ.

The Stone Table has global missions roots, and we believe the marketplace has implications on our calling to reach both our own communities and the ends of the earth with the resurrection

---

1   Os Hillman. "Is This Billy Graham Prophecy About the Next Great Move of God Coming to Pass?" *Charisma*. http://www.charismanews.com/marketplace/72688-is-this-billy-graham-prophecy-about-the-next-great-move-of-god-coming-to-pass (accessed April 13, 2021).

power of Jesus. This said, I humbly offer my perspective and stories that I hope will create a powerful gospel-collision between your faith, your work, and the global mission of God in this world. I long to see the marketplace redeemed and activated for the kingdom of God around the world.

Accelerating the Great Commission through the marketplace,

Erik Cooper

President of The Stone Table
Indianapolis, Indiana

INTRODUCTION

My church, my family, and the organizations we lead are laser-focused on global missions, something you will quickly pick up on in the pages that follow. It seems to me that most Christians who share our global missions priority don't talk much about work theology, and those who carry a robust theology of the marketplace put lesser emphasis on taking Jesus to the ends of the earth. It feels like these passions rarely coexist. Why is this?

In looking for a good way to articulate my conviction that these Kingdom passions most certainly do belong together, I started framing the faith and work discussion through three lenses. These three "greats" outline the three main sections of this book:

Part 1: Work and the Great Story. We start by looking through the lens of God's Great Story, the overarching narrative of the Bible. We don't invite God into our story; it is God who has invited us into His. When we frame our work inside His eternal and unfolding storyline, it changes everything. Here we explore the narrative of God's Word, a basic theology of work, and the Lord's Prayer from a marketplace perspective.

Part 2: Work and the Great Commandment. This section uses the lens of the Great Commandment: Love the Lord with all your heart, soul, and mind, and love your neighbor as yourself. Each day when the alarm clock goes off, you and I have the opportunity to honor God and love our neighbor with the work of our hands. We'll explore work as worship and service, the problem of greed, hiring and firing, rhythms of rest, and even retirement.

Part 3: Work and the Great Commission. Jesus' last instructions to His followers forms the third lens: Go, therefore, and make disciples of all nations. A call to the marketplace doesn't excuse us from Jesus' command to proclaim the gospel of His kingdom to the ends of the earth. In fact, the marketplace is a powerful cultural mechanism for fulfilling it. This third section offers some practical insight as to how marketplace believers can be obedient to Jesus' Great Commission calling.

Sprinkled throughout are stories of business as mission (BAM) practitioners, providing tangible examples of how these three "greats" are being embraced and lived out in the real world. These people are demonstrating and proclaiming Jesus from the marketplace in their local communities and around the world. I hope their stories encourage and inspire you.

I must confess, it's intimidating to step into this marketplace and mission conversation. Some of the most respected theological voices of our day—Timothy Keller, Os Guinness, Amy Sherman, Dick Brogden, just to name a few—have already said and written so much in such brilliant and illuminating ways. In fact, you will hear overtones, phraseology, and references to their incredible work throughout this book. These smart theologians and missiologists have unpacked this subject in ways I could never touch. They inspire and challenge me deeply. Please read them.

But I believe that as different voices share from their unique experiences and starting points, we bring more color and vibrancy to the broader Kingdom discussion. So, consider this book my humble, Midwestern, story-driven, business practitioner's contribution to what's often a deeply intellectual and theological conversation. My hope and my prayer are that this book stirs deep Kingdom meaning in the daily work God has called you to and ignites a passion for those who desperately need to know Jesus around the world.

CHAPTER

1

Setting the Stage

We make a living by what we get. We make
a life by what we give.

WINSTON CHURCHILL

M y parents moved from Philadelphia to Indianapolis in 1971 so my dad could begin a new job as a healthcare auditor for a local CPA firm. At that time, our beloved Midwestern city was better known as "Indiana-no-place." The downtown streets pretty much rolled up at dark as people retreated to their cornfield-enveloped housing developments on the outskirts of town.

My folks settled into Midwestern life, bought a house, plugged into a great church, and started a family (me, followed by my younger brother ten years later). My dad was good at his job, but the long hours and meager salary got him thinking.

One day he came home and told my mom, "I think I'm just as smart as the guys who own these healthcare facilities I'm auditing." So, he got up his nerve, found two business partners, borrowed a bunch of money, and started building what ultimately became a successful portfolio of nine nursing homes around the state of Indiana.

Skilled nursing care was a great business during the 1980s, but as the Reagan era drew to a close, shifts in the market caused them to reconsider their business plan. They sold out and started looking for new opportunities.

For my dad, that became partial ownership of a steakhouse on Indy's north side (not bad when you're a hungry teenager), an exclusive license to sell collector's pins during the 1987 Pan Am games, a stint in condominium development, and a few other investments he probably prefers I don't mention.

Where others might boast a brain full of unrealized ideas, my dad found the courage to recognize opportunities, step out, and actually make something where nothing existed before. He became a serial entrepreneur of sorts. But his ministry past still percolated in his DNA.

POOR PREACHER'S KID

My dad grew up as the son of a small-town pastor. My grandfather's legacy was faithfully leading small congregations up and down the East Coast of the U.S. Sometimes the church had actual money for his salary, and sometimes they would pay him in chickens. *Live* chickens. My dad has vivid memories of my grandpa and his ax "prepping" dinner on an old tree stump out back and literally watching as a "chicken with its head cut off" ran around the backyard.

My dad didn't want us growing up that way.

Poor.

He set out in a different vocational journey, but one I believe was equally divine (even though at the time he would have never thought of it that way). My dad had a natural intuition for finance and entrepreneurship, and his goal from the time he was a young business student at Evangel College in Springfield, Missouri was to one day have a million dollars in the bank. That's a big number today, but it was even bigger in 1960s. The Lord then spent the next thirty-five years regencrating that seemingly self-centered passion for something more eternal.

You see, even though my dad didn't share my grandfather's call into *ecclesiastical* (pastoral) ministry, the roots of Kingdom impact were still budding deep in his soul. Even though he couldn't articulate it then, a sacred calling to the marketplace drove him forward.

SLOW BAKED IN THE GREAT COMMISSION

We attended a church with a passion for global missions. I like to say that we "slow baked" in the Great Commission.

The front parking lot boasted the flags of the nations, which surrounded a large sandstone monument inscribed with the phrase, "Touching our world with His hands." A giant globe sat atop a flowing fountain full of spare change in the main lobby. Pictures of over three hundred missionaries lined the wood-paneled walls of the church. But that was just the décor.

Nearly every Sunday featured a short speaking window for an itinerating missionary sharing exotic and supernatural stories of the gospel's spread to the far reaches of the globe. Annual missions "conventions" put missionary families in our homes, offered "taste of missions" smorgasbords in the fellowship hall after service, and culminated with a Disney-esque parade of nations that celebrated God's work among the vast and diverse cultures of the world.

Throw all of this into a stew—pastor's kid, love for missions, knack for business—and this entrepreneur who grew up sacrificing his childhood bed to itinerating missionaries was prepared for a divinely explosive new season of life.

A PURPOSEFUL NEW SEASON

As the big hair of the '80s gave way to the Chicago Bulls dynasty of the '90s, my dad was an unsettled entrepreneur looking for his next opportunity.

Our long-time pastor, Tom Paino, was preparing for retirement after forty-plus years of church ministry. His global missions passion would not retire with him though; instead, in life after pastoring he became a high-impact missions fundraiser for priority Kingdom projects around the world.

At the same time, a brilliant young real estate developer was also sitting under Pastor Tom's Great Commission leadership. Tim Shrout was already making his mark developing and managing real estate around the Midwest when he learned of a new program the Federal Government was starting in order to preserve its affordable housing inventory.

At the time much of the nation's affordable housing portfolio was built by for-profit developers in the 1960s and '70s. These developers made twenty-year commitments to the government in exchange for Section 8 contracts and lower-than-market interest rates. However, by the early 1990s these affordability commitments were starting to run out, and many owners were already making plans to convert the properties to market-rate communities, put in higher-end amenities, and raise rents to levels lower-income people couldn't afford.

The government started a grant program to incentivize non-profits to purchase these properties from their for-profit owners. In exchange, these non-profits committed to keep them affordable forever. It was a public-private partnership aimed at creating a sustainable business model that would solve a looming national crisis. *Opportunity knocks!*

Tim began dreaming of a non-profit housing company that would leverage this grant program to build a strategic new real estate portfolio. Not only could the new business help sustain affordable housing for people who need it, but these newly acquired assets could also generate cashflow that could then be dedicated to priority global missions initiatives.

THE MARKETPLACE AND THE MISSION OF GOD

This missional business concept excited Tim so much he nearly left his other endeavors to pursue it full-time, but ultimately, he decided to approach my dad with the idea. Our families were friends and had attended church together for some time. My dad was assisting Tim's company with a few nursing home transactions while he looked for his next opportunity. Over lunch one day, Tim unfolded the creative business model he was dreaming of, and the concept ignited something supernatural in my dad as well. Together, Tim and my dad became the co-founders and legacy board members of Community Reinvestment Foundation, Inc. (or CRF).

My dad eagerly tackled the day-to-day development of this newly formed entity. Unknown to many (including my mom), he funded the initial operating costs with a personal line of credit on my childhood home. Nonprofit or not, entrepreneurs are just compelled to bring important things to life.

Thankfully, CRF's start-up costs were lean. Our initial "world headquarters" was a borrowed office provided by the church. The "executive suite" doubled as the counting room and storage closet for the church safe, making Mondays a mandatory day off while the church completed the weekly offering count. Even CRF's first official staff member, Dwayne Shaw, was initially "borrowed" from Tim Shrout's organization to help close the early real estate transactions. It was far from glamorous, but something beautiful was brewing.

From day one, CRF was designed so that half its annual profits would go back into growing the business while the other half went right out the door to strategic global missions projects through Pastor Tom's fundraising organization called ActioNow. Those early calculations were easy as half of zero is not a complicated math problem. But do not despise the days of small beginnings (Zechariah 4:10).

The company grew slowly through the years, but not without its share of difficulty and conflict. After a year of hard work and nineteen properties in the pipeline, the government abruptly canceled the grant program leaving CRF with enormous dreams but only one property. Thankfully, Tim Shrout stepped in once again to help secure a large third-party management contract that gave the fledgling start-up some hope. Over the next few years, CRF methodically began to negotiate the purchase of these fee-managed properties, and by the early 2000s, the company was finally on solid ground.

> **"Do not despise the days of small beginnings."**
>
> ZECH. 4:10

Through slow and steady leadership, prayerful problem solving, and a consistent commitment to give away half the profits each year to Kingdom work, CRF finally became a stable affordable housing provider and began generating steady returns for global missions work each year.

STANDING ON THE SHOULDERS OF GIANTS

In 2012, I came on board at CRF after a twelve-year season in full-time pastoral ministry. My original background was business, my experience was ministry, and the future of CRF was in need of someone who could uniquely straddle both worlds. I remain grateful and honored to have received that call.

Shortly after, Pastor Tom (now in his late 90s) made it clear that it was time to pass the global missions mantle as well. We launched The Stone Table, a sister-company to CRF, to take the missions baton from Pastor Tom after decades of strategic missions fundraising work. My brother-in-law David Wigington, a long-time pastor and brilliant missions fundraiser, now walks alongside me as a board member and powerful multiplier of our missions efforts.

For context, The Stone Table name is a reference to C. S. Lewis and *The Chronicles of Narnia*. It's the location of the death and resurrection of Aslan, the Christ character, and a daily reminder that everything we do here, from the marketplace to the mission field, must remain centered on the good news of Jesus Christ.

Tables are also gathering places, and The Stone Table has become a "gospel gathering place" of sorts. We bring together entrepreneurs and pastors, business leaders and missionaries, all for the sake of the gospel around the world. To date, we have raised and given well over $15 million dollars for missions work around the world through our business and through church and marketplace partners. As daily stewards of a successful business model, we find joy in calling others to give *with* us instead of *to* us.

BEYOND MONEY ALONE

From the start, our heart has been to mobilize marketplace believers beyond money alone. Most entrepreneurs, business owners, and Christians with marketplace occupations have been encouraged to give financially. *And that should continue!* Financial generosity is a vital part of God's kingdom mission and calling for all of us. We must give—and give *sacrificially.*

However, we firmly believe that a holistic work theology illuminates a much richer calling for marketplace believers than signing checks alone. As marketplace Christians ourselves, we feel a deep longing to educate, empower, coach, and release marketplace Christians into their fully intended vocation within God's kingdom story.

That's what this book is about. I want to take you on a gospel-empowering journey from my seat as a business leader. I want to get under the surface, harvest the Kingdom seeds that drove the creation of our company, explore them through the lens of God's Word, and plant them in as many other marketplace Christians as possible.

How do we find our own vocational stories within the context of God's Great Story? How do we reimagine our everyday work through the paradigm of the Great Commandment? How do we harness the power of the marketplace to fulfill the Great

Commission? I will attempt to pull together a wide variety of marketplace and ministry ideas, from how the gospel redeems and resurrects your own job, to how the marketplace is uniquely positioned to demonstrate and proclaim the name of Jesus to the ends of the earth.

Like Billy Graham, I believe that releasing Christians in the workplace to their full Kingdom potential could be the genesis of the next great awakening in our world. Before we talk about the beautiful ways this is already happening, I want to spend some time undoing a few common and foundational misunderstandings about our everyday work and its role in God's kingdom. Grab your sleeping bag and your bug spray; we're heading off to summer camp.

2

The Sacred–Secular Divide

The spiritual manifests itself in a life which
knows no division into sacred and secular.

OSWALD CHAMBERS

I spent a week at church camp every summer when I was a kid. Some of the most formative God-encounters of my young faith happened in the old, rusted-out metal airplane hangar that served as the campground sanctuary.

Hartford City, Indiana was hardly the urban center its name tries to imply. One of the most memorable features of the "city," aside from the sprawling Assemblies of God campground that covered eighty-five of its acres, was the smell. The water table in this rural, Midwestern farming community contained abnormally high levels of sulfur, adding a faint scent of rotten eggs to the natural odor of three hundred smelly teenagers.

Imagine spending the day participating in high-energy camp competitions only to return to the dorm for a sulfur-water shower before heading to dinner and the evening church service. Nothing attracts the opposite sex quite like the musk of rotting breakfast food.

The evening services were long but powerful. The corrugated metal hangar that served as our sanctuary was undergirded by a concrete floor and furnished with metal folding chairs. A good Midwestern summer thunderstorm would resonate off the hard surfaces with deafening ferocity, but nothing could drown out the passion of the charismatic services and extended times praying and worshipping around the altar with hundreds of other high school students. God truly moved in our lives during those humid July evenings.

The perennial theme of summer church camp was Zechariah 4:6. I can still see the vinyl banner hanging over the makeshift platform. It read, "Not by might, nor by power, but by my Spirit, says the Lord Almighty" (NIV).

But within that larger vision, each night of church camp always had a theme of its own. Monday night was a strong salvation message intended to flush out those imposters who were there because their parents made them go. Tuesday was usually about living holy lives in a sinful world, pushing all of us to go deeper in our relationship with Jesus. Wednesday explored the empowerment of the Holy Spirit.

And then came Thursday. Blessed Thursday.

"CALLED INTO MINISTRY" NIGHT

The final service always brought the crescendo of summer camp with "called into ministry" night. The camp evangelist preached a powerful message on what it meant to be *called* into full-time ministry, and the sermon climaxed with a gut-check question: Who here feels like God is calling them into the ministry?

Inevitably, about ten percent of the kids raised their hands. Future pastors. Future missionaries. The Lord was stirring the hearts of these young followers and preparing them for a life of service to the kingdom of God.

Then the evangelist invited these newly called candidates to the front and gathered them around the altars. After waiting a few moments for the stragglers, the remaining ninety percent of us were asked to leave our metal folding chairs, too, to stand behind and lay our hands on the shoulders and heads of our newly called friends. We prayed long, passionate prayers over those who were called, sang a few celebratory songs, and then headed back to our seats as some called by God into the ministry and the rest of us just destined for "secular work."

This was the exact terminology we used: Called into ministry. Going into secular work.

I remember friends hollering at me from across the snack shop after service, "Hey, Coop, did you get it? Did you get *the call?*"

"No, no, I didn't," I would annually retort. "I'm *just* going into a secular work. Business maybe."

Just.

Secular.

Work.

In seeking to clarify the ecclesiastical (pastoral) calling on people's lives, we were unwittingly segregating the way we thought about Christian work and calling as a whole.

Please don't get me wrong. There is something unequivocally unique about the distinct ecclesiastical call into full-time ministry work (I ultimately ended up spending twelve years in that vital role myself). But the unfortunate, and I believe unintended, theological byproduct was an assumed separation between what is sacred and what is secular, and the result is a vast majority of Christians who think their work has little to nothing to do with the work of God. To this day, many of us still unwittingly carry this bad work theology into our everyday jobs.

In risk of revisiting those awkward middle school years, let's head back to the junior high lunchroom for some further explanation.

THE PARABLE OF THE LUNCH TRAY

I hated my food touching when I was a kid. There is an actual psychological term for this: *brumotactillophobia.*

It sounds more like a giant reptile from the Cretaceous period than a psychological disorder. Doctors place it in the family of obsessive-compulsive. A lot of young kids have this. My psychosis has followed me into adulthood, because let's be honest, there is *nothing* worse than the juice from your green beans seeping into your mashed potatoes (literally gagging as I write that.)

Because of this irrational bent, I became very fond of those plastic lunch trays from elementary school. You remember those? The ones that had the walled compartments for each individual food group—a big rectangle for the Salisbury steak, a smaller square for the mashed potatoes, a little circle for those canned peaches (in heavy syrup), and that special little square with the inset circle made for the milk carton. This, my friends, is how all food should be served in an advanced civilization.

While these partitioned trays are perfect for battling *brumotactillophobia,* they're a horrible analogy for how we think about our Christian lives. Yet the majority of Western evangelicals seem to have embraced the idea that certain sections of our lives are for sacred activities, and others are reserved for the secular.

This may surprise you, but that middle school lunch tray approach to the Christian life is actually a modern form of ancient Gnosticism. Simply stated, the Gnostics (from *gnosis,* the Greek word for "knowledge") believed that spiritual things were good and physical matter was evil. They segregated all aspects of life into different buckets—some sacred and others secular.

This Christian dualism, or the partitioning of our lives into sacred and secular components, is actually a heresy the church has been fighting since the second century, and we aren't immune today. Here's how we might verbalize these Gnostic tendencies in our modern context:

- I work for a CPA firm. That's my *secular* job. But I volunteer in kids' church on Sundays. That is my *ministry*.
- I work for a construction company by day, but that's just my *secular* work. I lead a small group at my church and that is where I engage in *real* ministry.
- I do graphic design work. That's my *secular* gig. But I sing on the worship team every other Sunday. That's my sacred *calling*.

In much of the Christian world today, there is an instinctive partitioning of life, a sacred-secular divide, that defines the work we do for the church as sacred and the work we do in the marketplace as secular. This is simply bad theology, an "abbreviation" of the full and glorious redemption narrative of the gospel.

Good work theology starts with reminding ourselves of the whole gospel. Look at Paul's liberating encouragement to the church in Colossae:

> *For God in all his fullness was pleased to live in Christ, and through him God **reconciled everything** to himself. He **made peace with everything** in heaven and on earth by means of Christ's blood on the cross. (Colossians 1:19–20 NLT, emphasis mine)*

The sacred nature of work is not just for pastors and those employed by the church. It is intended for *all* Christians! Through Jesus, God reconciled and made peace with all things. There is not one aspect of our lives that the gospel does not redeem. Jesus didn't just come to resurrect the "sacred partitions" of my life; He came to redeem my *whole lunch tray*!

This blessed gospel, the good news of Jesus Christ, is actively renewing, redeeming, and resurrecting all things, including the work of our hands. This is liberating news! Let's unpack this one more way.

> *"The sacred nature of work... is intended for all Christians."*

WHAT IS YOUR VOCATION?

What do you think of when you hear the word "vocation"? Vocation, the term we use to describe someone's career or what they do for a living, has its root in the Latin word *vocare*. And guess what that means...

Calling.

For the Christian, this is an incredibly empowering discovery. Throughout his writing, the Apostle Paul used this exact same word to describe all kinds of work: work inside the church, work in the home, and work in the marketplace. Imagine what the altars on Thursday night at church camp would have looked like under that definition! Here's one example from Paul:

Only let each person lead the life that the Lord has
***assigned** to him, and to which God has **called** him. (1*
Corinthians 7:17, emphasis mine)

Tim Keller illuminates this so well in his faith-and-work masterpiece, *Every Good Endeavor:* "Here Paul uses two religiously freighted words to describe ordinary work. Elsewhere, Paul has spoken of God calling people into a saving relationship with him, and assigning them spiritual gifts to do ministry and build up the Christian community (Romans 12:3 and 2 Corinthians 10:13). Paul uses these same two words here when he says that every Christian should remain in the work God has 'assigned to him, and to which God has called him.' Yet Paul is not referring in this case to church ministries, but to common social and economic tasks— 'secular jobs,' we might say—and naming them God's callings and assignments."[2]

This is game-changing news, my fellow believer. Your work, whether you're a teacher, a software engineer, a banker, a builder, an attorney (I know, hard to believe, but *even* an attorney!), a factory worker, an entrepreneur, a stay-at-home mom, blue collar, white collar, esteemed or humble, if you're a pediatrician or you work the deli counter at the supermarket *and* you are reconciled to Christ, your work is a sacred calling!

Let me say that again.

In Christ. Your. Work. Is. Sacred.

---

2   Timothy Keller. *Every Good Endeavor.* New York City: Penguin Books, 2014. 55.

Have you ever thought about your day job like that? It's time.

The gospel does away with the heretical concept of "secular work." Jesus is reconciling and redeeming *all* things, including your day job. You don't have a secular job, my friend; you have a sacred calling.

Now that we've undone some bad theology, let's explore the powerful, gospel-regenerated potential of our everyday work.

PART

I

Work and the Great Story

And for us this is the end of all the stories,
and we can most truly say that they all lived
happily ever after. But for them it was only
the beginning of the real story. All their life in
this world and all their adventures in Narnia
had only been the cover and the title page:
now at last they were beginning Chapter One
of the Great Story which no one on earth has
read: which goes on forever: in which every
chapter is better than the one before.

C. S. LEWIS, *THE LAST BATTLE*

CHAPTER

3

A Gospel Revolution

[We] are not being led to see God in our
stories, but to see our stories in God's.

EUGENE PETERSON

N icolaus was born into a well-to-do family in Torún, Poland.
His father was a successful businessman who passed
away unexpectedly when Nicolaus was just 10. Nicolaus' mother,
believing he needed the influence of a strong male figure in his
life, sent him to live with her brother in a nearby town. Nicolaus'
uncle was a pastor and respected community leader, and he took
responsibility for Nicolaus' education and upbringing from that
day forward.

Nicolaus' uncle made certain that he attended college, and
his initial studies covered a wide range of subjects including
art, math, religion, and the humanities. He was adamant that

Nicolaus would carry the family name forward in a way that made everyone proud.

Nicolaus had a side fascination with outer space. He could not stop staring at the stars! His growing passion for astronomy sucked him in, like the gravitational pull of the sun, and he began collecting every kind of book on the subject and spent all his spare time consuming anything he could find in the field of this celestial obsession.

While skipping his religion classes one day, Nicolaus met and became fast friends with an experienced astronomer who began mentoring him. Nicolaus worked as his informal apprentice, and before long, the two began using their mathematical calculations to challenge a fundamental astronomical theory.

The theory they challenged—that earth was the center of the universe.

Even though this "heliocentric model of the universe" was proposed as early as the third century B.C., Nicolaus Copernicus was the one to finally prove it. The book containing the final version of his theory appeared in printed form in 1543, the same year he died.

It was the discovery that disrupted *everything*.

No longer could human beings see themselves and their world as the center of all things, the constant that everything else revolved around. On a foundational, scientific level, we had to face the unsettling fact that our entire existence is supported by a tiny, spinning, almost inconsequential mass floating in an immeasurably vast, unexplored universe.

It was a humbling declaration to say the least. Proof or no proof, people did not like it. And I mean *no one,* not one person. Revisionist history likes to frame this story solely as a battle between factual science and superstitious religion. And while it's true that the Catholic Church did ban Copernicus' work for over two hundred years, this was not an anti-science power play by a group of religious zealots.

The truth is that no one believed the earth revolved around the sun. It just wasn't an observable reality. It wasn't logical. And it probably just didn't feel right either. The Copernican Revolution didn't just change the science of astronomy; it changed how we humans see ourselves in relationship to a much greater whole.

WE NEED A COPERNICAN REVOLUTION

One of the reasons we struggle to write a great life story, and ultimately to find meaning in our work, even as Christians, is because we still see ourselves as the center of our own story.

That's understandable. I see the world through my lens, through my eyes, through my experiences. Every camera shot is from my perspective. I am the main character of my movie. The rest of you are just my supporting cast, today's "crowd extras." I'm thankful for you, but if you come or go, if your part is written in or out of my script, it may have a peripheral impact on the narrative, but it doesn't change the fact that my story is propelled forward by me.

I'm grateful for your help and all, but it's *my face* on the movie poster. I'll be the one signing the autographs.

You're likely saying the same thing, maybe not overtly, but intuitively. Our sin nature puts the "self" at the center of everything. The rest of the world exists to revolve around us. This is the "secular religion" of our age.

Modern philosopher Charles Taylor refers to these ideals as "closed world structures," a framework for our lives that eliminates all transcendence and belief that anything is greater than the self. These "axiomatic truths" are simply the stories we tell ourselves about ourselves.[3] We see them, both subtly and overtly, in everything from movies to children's stories to funny memes floating around the internet. "Always be true to yourself" and "never sacrifice your happiness for anyone else" are two of modern culture's most cherished statements of faith.

So, when it comes to our work, our job, our career, our everyday tasks, the vision of the good life we have for our future, the primary questions we inherently ask are:

- Does this work fit the story I am writing about myself?
- Does it fulfill me?
- Does it make me happy?
- Does it give me worth?
- Does it earn me respect?
- Does it give me more power and autonomy?
- Does it fit my identity and the way I want to see myself?

---

3   Charles Taylor. *A Secular Age.* Boston: Harvard University Press, 2007.

And since nothing outside of God Himself can truly carry the ultimate weight of our identity and happiness, the answer is always no.

When it comes to our everyday work, we desperately need a Copernican Revolution, or rather, a Gospel Revolution. We are not the main characters in a story that we're writing about ourselves. Instead, we are beloved members of the supporting cast in a divine, cosmic narrative God has been unfolding since the beginning of time.

> **"Our lives are beautiful, little subplots created to revolve around the Great Story of the Creator Himself."**

It's time to flip the script. We've been invited into an epic story, but just like Copernicus, it requires a reversal of who we see at the center. We will never find fulfillment and meaning in our daily work until we place our stories inside God's story. Our lives are beautiful, little subplots created to revolve around the Great Story of the Creator Himself. We will only find joy and purpose in our work when we place that work—and the entirety of our lives—inside Him.

WHO LIVES, WHO DIES, WHO TELLS HIS STORY?

Let me illustrate this point with a pop culture detour. Like much of the world, my family became infatuated (perhaps mildly obsessed) with the musical *Hamilton*. We had heard all the hype, but until Disney released it to the adulation of the COVID-quarantined masses in July 2020, we didn't really understand.

While the old-school prude in me found some of the salty language a bit unnecessary, you cannot deny the genius of Lin-Manuel Miranda's masterpiece. History, artistry, and pop culture collide in two and a half hours of surprisingly solid historical education and emotional storytelling. It's quite the ride.

The first time I watched it, I missed some of the incredible minutiae imbedded in the high-speed rap and spoken word, but the soundtrack consistently accompanied our family on car rides for weeks. With each listen, I grasped more of the storyline and it sucked me deeper into the humanity of our nation's founding.

The musical culminates with the moving song "Who Lives, Who Dies, Who Tells Your Story?" It brings a haunting resolution to this chronicle of an ambitious orphan immigrant who willed himself to become one of our nation's most influential founding fathers. Alexander Hamilton desperately wanted to matter in this life, and he leveraged all of his passion to make sure his name would be forever etched in our history books. Almost 250 years later, we're still retelling his story in books, on monuments, and now eight times a week at Richard Rogers Theater in New York City.

A LONGING WE ALL SHARE

It's a longing all of us share in some way, isn't it?

To matter.

To be remembered.

To have our efforts live on long after we're gone.

It's actually part of our original design. Check this out:

> *And God blessed them. And God said to them, "Be fruitful and multiply and fill the earth and subdue it, and have dominion over the fish of the sea and over the birds of the heavens and over every living thing that moves on the earth." (Genesis 1:28)*

We were created to subdue and have dominion (we will explore this more in Chapter 5). It isn't just hubris. We were made to be co-creators, image-bearers, vice-regents of God Almighty. We were created to do things that matter, important things, things that echo into eternity. That deep longing for transcendence is baked into our God-given DNA.

It's just been hijacked by sin.

And so instead of spending our days subduing and having dominion under God and to His glory, we strive to make a name for ourselves and to build monuments to our own fame. We endeavor to write stories that will keep people talking about us and our contributions. Maybe I can be interesting enough that someone will want to write a musical about me one day, too. (You never know, right?) We go searching for that legendary storyline in the next relationship, that elusive dream-job, or the "likes" and "hearts" of the trendiest social media platform. Most of us never get there, and those who think they do find out their self-made immortality still leaves them empty and wanting.

Because while we were made to tell an epic story, the story we're to tell has never been our own.

THERE IS ONE STORY TO TELL

I love how N. T. Wright frames the question in *The New Testament in Its World:* "How do we understand the play, the real-life story of God and the world which reached its ultimate climax in Jesus of Nazareth and which then flows out, in the power of the spirit, to transform the world with his love and justice? How do we find our own parts and learn to play them? How do we let the poetry of the early Christians, whether it's the short and dense poems we find in Paul or the extended fantasy-literature of the book of Revelation, transform our imaginations so that we can start to think in new ways about God and the world, about the powers that still threaten darkness and death, and about our role in implementing the victory of Jesus?"[4]

You and I have a story to tell. Whether we are plumbers, farmers, Wall Street stockbrokers, missionaries, waiters, accountants, pastors, CEOs, or small business owners, our story has a vital role in a much larger epic story that is not our own. How we're

4   N. T. Wright. *The New Testament in Its World: An Introduction to the History, Literature, and Theology of the First Christians.* Grand Rapids, MI: Zondervan Academic, 2019.

remembered or whether we're remembered at all really isn't the satisfying objective.

When Jesus cried "It is finished!" from the cross, He made the final declaration that in Him we are loved and immeasurably valuable and that we matter for all eternity. When that finished work of Christ finally seeps in and fills those cracks in the deepest longings of our souls, then we will gladly allow our stories to get lost in the Great Story of God where it beautifully belongs and finds its true meaning.

When I listen to the closing track of *Hamilton*, I can't help but get a little emotional. I feel the soul ache of a poor orphan kid who just wants to matter to somebody in this world. I feel the deep pain of his wife, Eliza, wanting to make sure no one ever forgets the vital contributions her husband made to the newly formed American experiment. And I feel the longing of each one of us, too, who live with a deep longing to be known, cherished, and ultimately remembered.

Then I remember the promises of the gospel. Everything I need in Christ I already have. With that foundational reality settled, I can finally embrace my supporting cast role in the Great Story my life was meant to tell, whether anyone remembers my name or not.

Who lives, who dies, who tells your story? That's a fleeting counterfeit.

Who lives, who dies, who tells His story? That is where life finds its designed meaning and purpose.

If our lives, including our everyday work, were created to exist inside a greater narrative, what is that Great Story? Next up is a whirlwind journey through 1,300 years of God's storytelling genius.

– *Business Consulting* –

I first met Tom at a gathering of BAM-minded leaders in Minneapolis. We spent some time during the breaks getting to know each other and our business backgrounds. Tom was right in the middle of selling the marketing business he founded over two decades earlier. He and his wife, an experienced IT manager, felt a distinct call to global missions work, but they wanted to leverage their extensive marketplace background in a strategic way.

Tom knew business as mission was in their future, but he had no idea where or how. We talked a few times in the months that followed, traded some network connections in the BAM sphere, and dreamed about where Tom and Patti's unique skillset could be best used for the Kingdom in a global context. Ultimately, Tom and I ended up as teachers on the same conference schedule for a gathering of BAM missionary practitioners in Europe.

I had the joy of listening to Tom teach transformational marketing concepts to dozens of missionaries leading missional businesses all over Europe, China, and the Arab world. His rich knowledge base, rooted in decades of real-life business experience, gave these BAM teams access to a new set of skills they would have paid thousands of dollars for on the open market.

Today, Tom and his wife are based overseas providing ongoing support and consultation for a growing number of strategic BAM businesses across the globe. All of the years Tom spent in the Minneapolis marketplace are being renewed and repurposed for a very strategic second act.

We are seeing these kinds of second careers everywhere as businesspeople of all levels and backgrounds are realizing their marketplace and entrepreneurial skillsets are vital to the global missions landscape today. Maybe Tom's story resonates with you. Even if God isn't asking you to live cross-culturally, your business skills are sacred to God and vital to His Great Commission calling. Is it time to prayerfully dream about what's next?

4

Origins and Endings

Superheroes were born in the minds of
people desperate to be rescued.

JODI PICOULT

S uperhero series often turn back the clock to show us the
origins of the characters and their storylines. These prequels
give us context we wouldn't otherwise have, adding new texture
and nuance to the narrative, which helps us understand the
greater story as a whole.

The same is true of you and me. If we're going to place ourselves
inside this Great Story of God, what exactly is the story, what is
the prequel? To understand our current role, including why we get
up and go to work each day, we need to understand the Author's
original intent. Where did this Great Story start, and where is it

ultimately taking us? We call this the metanarrative of Scripture, the overarching storyline of the Bible.

It's easy to approach the Bible as a book of spiritual advice. If we want to understand what God thinks about money, parenting, or politics—or in our case here, our everyday marketplace work—we grab our Bibles and search for characters, verses, and scriptural accounts that might give us some insight into God's take on that topic. But God isn't selling the latest self-help craze, and Scripture isn't peddling five ways to get thin in Jesus in thirty days. That's just another way of putting "me" at the center of my story all over again. When we look at the Bible through our perspective and experiences, we miss the ultimate point. When we look at our lives through the lens of God's story, a resurrected world begins to appear in vibrant color and new dimensions.

The Bible is not a topical encyclopedia of spiritual advice. The Bible is primarily a story—the Great Story that God has been unfolding since before the beginning of time, a story we have all been invited into through His Son Jesus. We'll unpack all the ways our everyday work fits into this narrative in the next chapter. For now, we'll stay zoomed out and establish some broader context.

THE GREAT STORY IN FOUR MAIN ACTS

If the Bible is really a story and not just a book of nice religious instruction, what is this story? The Bible crafts this metanarrative through sixty-six books written over 1,500 years. I'm going to attempt to synopsize here it in a few paragraphs.

Theologians typically compile the Great Story into four main acts. Sometimes you will see the segments titled differently, but the content is the same.

Act 1: Creation

In the beginning was God. He has no origin and no ending. He exists outside our understanding of space and time. He was perfect and complete in and of Himself. Yet He longed to share His love, so God created the heavens and the earth (Genesis 1:1).

As the crowning jewel of His new world, God breathed life into man and woman and set us inside His new creation. He didn't need you and me, but He wanted you and me.

His plan was to dwell with us. The earth itself was the original temple, the meeting place of God and His beloved creation. God Himself physically walked with man in the garden in the cool of the day (Genesis 3:8). Just like a chalice crafted to be filled with the sweetest wine, His creation was made to be filled with the fullness of His glory.[5]

Eden was a perfect paradise, and not just because it was green, lush, and pristine, but because God Himself literally dwelled with mankind. Everything functioned as it was originally designed. This is our origin story: God's image-bearing creation living in the fullness of His loving presence, reflecting His glory, and fulfilling

---

5   N. T. Wright. *Surprised by Hope: Rethinking Heaven, the Resurrection, and the Mission of the Church.* San Francisco: HarperOne, 2007.

our human vocation to cultivate and care for His world. It is with God that we are fully alive and fully human.

Act 2: The Fall

But then something horrible happened that broke this perfect union.

Rebellion. Transgression. Sin.

Our desire to *be* God instead of *reflect* God severed our perfect union *with* God. The serpent said to our original ancestors:

> *God knows that your eyes will be opened as soon as you eat it, **and you will be like God**, knowing both good and evil. (Genesis 3:5 NLT, emphasis mine)*

Sin disconnected us from our designed union with our Creator and cursed all creation with physical separation from God.

> *But **your iniquities have made a separation** between you and your God, and your sins have hidden His face from you so that He does not hear. (Isaiah 59:2, emphasis mine)*

We had all that we needed in the presence of God Himself, but we leveraged our God-given free will to go searching for fulfillment and identity in everything except where we were created to find it—in *God Himself.*

This idolatry, this rejection of our original design as image-bearers is the root of all sin, so God aborted His original plan and cast mankind out of His presence, not only as punishment, but because our rebellion and His holiness are incapable of coexisting.

The dimension of God and the dimension of man no longer overlapped. We were left to function alone and disconnected from our Source. This absence of God's presence did not only affect mankind but all of creation, which now groans in painful longing for things to be made right once again (Romans 8:22). As C. S. Lewis wrote in *Chronicles of Narnia: The Lion, the Witch and the Wardrobe*, "it was always winter but never Christmas."

And yet, since Genesis 3, God has been passionately pursuing the reunification of this broken connection. The Great Story follows a loving Creator chasing down His beloved, lost, and wandering creation to restore the togetherness, that *with*-ness, for which we were made.

Act 3: Redemption

At first, God begins to break through this dimensional separation in very strategic and formal ways. This redemption act begins with a promise to a man named Abraham and a covenant agreement that all the people of the earth would be blessed through him (Genesis 12:2–3). Abraham's family grew into tribes and eventually multiplied into a great nation called Israel. All along the journey, this covenant promise grew with them.

Through Abraham and his offspring, God would reopen communication and connection with His lost and beloved world. Before sin, all of creation itself was the temple, the place where

God and man dwelled together in perfect union. Through the nation of Israel, God reopened a portal in our sin-made barrier and began to tabernacle with His people once again.

God's tangible presence hovered between the wings of the golden cherubim which sat atop the ark of the covenant (Exodus 25:22). This ark was hidden from the masses behind a special curtain, initially inside a mobile tent called the tabernacle and ultimately in the permanent temple structure when Israel entered the Promised Land. The Law was given as a temporary placeholder outlining the expectations for a holy life, and sin was dealt with through a series of animal sacrifices and offerings.

But all of this was just a foreshadow of the glory to come! God's plan was always for a permanent solution to redeem all creation and re-establish His kingdom "on earth as it is in heaven." God's presence was ready to break through the sin barrier once and for all.

Enter Jesus, the perfect and final sacrifice for our sin. When Jesus died on the cross, the temple curtain that separated the people from the presence of God was torn in two, and His bodily resurrection established the firstfruits of a fully renewed creation. God's grace burst into the world through Christ, reawakening all those who put their faith and trust in Him. Jesus brought back to life all that sin had destroyed.

Through faith, Jesus now lives in us. God's presence is no longer housed in a temple made of stone. He resides in human hearts.

But that's not the final act.

Act 4: Restoration

Through Christ, God and man can once again be reunited!

> *Do you not know that **you are God's temple** and that **God's Spirit dwells in you?** (1 Corinthians 3:16, emphasis mine)*

> *Jesus answered him, "If anyone loves me, he will keep my word, and my Father will love him, and **we will come to him and make our home with him**." (John 14:23, emphasis mine)*

God is restoring all things to Himself through Jesus, and in Christ, we have now become the first taste of His coming kingdom (James 1:18). We are the "buds on the trees announcing that spring is coming!"

We live in the great overlap, a chapter in this Great Story known as the "already but not yet." A foretaste of the Kingdom is here, but the whole Kingdom is coming! He is refilling the sin-empty chalice and restoring His rule here on earth in and through His people, those who by faith willfully surrender and reorder their lives around the finished work of Jesus.

One day, Jesus will physically return again and complete this Great Story. God and man will fully dwell together again as originally designed. Look where this is going:

> *Behold, **the dwelling place of God is with man.** He will dwell **with them,** and they will be his people, and God*

*himself will be **with them** as their God.* (Revelation 21:3, emphasis mine)

WORK AND THE GREAT STORY

Okay, so we've grasped the grand narrative. But what in the world could this story possibly have to do with our day jobs, our careers, our everyday work?

In a word...

Everything!

This is the Great Story you and I have been *re*-born into, and it's the grand narrative in which all of our stories, great or small, find their ultimate purpose and meaning. God is not Someone we invite into our stories—we have been gloriously invited into His!

Your ambitions, dreams, wiring, giftings, passions—all of them are God-given. But they were made to be derivative. We bear the image of Another. We are caretakers and stewards of our Redeemer's storyline, not our own. We aren't made to be gods; we are made to reflect God. We are beloved and cherished members of the supporting cast. This is where we find our purpose, our meaning, our joy, and our calling.

Our day jobs are not about selfish ambition or self-actualization, accumulating power, earning the respect and admiration of others, making our mark on the world, or becoming famous and well-known. Ultimately, our work is not about us at all. Our stories are divinely crafted subplots in the great, cosmic redemption story of God! It's into this story that our small stories, including our everyday work, find their true meaning and place.

"Ultimately, our work is not about us at all."

We know our origin and we know the ending, where it began and where it's all going. It's inside the unfolding narrative of this Great Story that we are fully alive!

– *Church Planting –*
Through Coffee

In a small, mountain community in one of the most unreached corners of China, a group of business as mission (BAM) workers are using coffee to demonstrate and proclaim the gospel to people who have never heard of Jesus before. China is a tea culture, but coffee is a new and fast-growing market. This has created a strategic BAM opportunity.

Through the daily presence of a local coffee shop, our friends are serving the community and fostering human connections. The business has become a hub for many regulars, and their consistent visits eventually turn into conversations about life. A few have already found Christ, and a small underground church has been born through a business model.

Beyond the retail store alone, the entire business supply chain is providing a beautiful channel for the gospel. The team also owns a local roastery that supplies the coffee shop with product. That roastery sources its raw beans from the rural mountain communities in the area, communities filled with unreached people groups.

Because of China's restrictive Communist policies, these workers aren't allowed to travel to these areas and interact with these people without a valid reason. The coffee business provides them just that. Multiple times per year, the team take trips into the mountains, not only to buy product for their business, but to interact with the people, foster relationships, and build trust. These are all beautiful byproducts of business done well, and over time, they become channels for gospel conversations as well.

As a coffee lover myself, I've always embraced coffee as a divine gift! But in this case, the gospel is finding its way into an unreached part of the world through the work of a local coffee shop and supply chain with strategic Kingdom intent. This is just one of many ways God is redeeming the marketplace for the Great Commission around the world.

5

Theology of Work 101

We're going to serve in eternity. We're not going to sit around on clouds; you know this whole idea [that] heaven is wearing white robes with angels and [playing] a harp. To me, that would be hell. I can't think of anything more boring.

RICK WARREN

No one intentionally taught me about God's design and purpose for work. It was more of an assumed theology, ideas inferred from other biblical teaching, a mix of what I observed from my dad and other Christians who worked in the marketplace and even from popular culture itself.

I don't know about you, but I grew up with a Sunday school flannelgraph image of what life must have been like before sin came into the world. I imagined Adam and Eve in the Garden of Eden laying in the lush grass next to a flowing stream covered with strategically placed fig leaves. What else was there to do, right? The Garden of Eden was a kick-back-and-relax zone. All leisure, all the time. Honestly, I assumed it probably got a little boring after a while, but that's what paradise is all about, right? The perfect extended vacation.

These assumptions led to what I like to call Looney Toons Theology.

Back when cartoons were mostly confined to Saturday mornings, classic Warner Brother's characters like Bugs Bunny, Daffy Duck, and Porky Pig ruled the airwaves. These cartoons were famously politically incorrect and filled with all kinds of cartoonish violence. Wile E. Coyote was probably the most brutalized victim, although his obsessive pursuit of the Road Runner rarely left you feeling much sympathy for him. I uncovered a fabulous article on the internet from a humane animal trapping company called Havahart. They analyzed all forty Road Runner episodes and determined the coyote somehow survived 341 fatal accidents, including ninety-five falls from long distances, seventy-three explosions, twelve boulders to the head, and three electrocutions. In the cartoon's second episode, which originally aired in 1952, the coyote should have died twenty times![6]

---

6   "Catch Me if You Can!" Havahart company website blog. https://www.havahart. com/catch-me-if-you-can (accessed April 28, 2021).

Resurrection is much easier when you're a cartoon, but occasionally a Warner Brother's character would actually meet his demise (at least until the next episode). I have vivid memories of a winged Elmer Fudd (following a "wascally wabbit" hunting mishap, no doubt) floating into the sky on a white puffy cloud with a halo on his head and a harp in his hands.

This imagery stuck.

My Sunday School flannelgraph memories told me God made humans to hang out all day in a permanent state of leisure.

My Saturday morning cartoon memories told me that when we die, our disembodied spirits will float up to heaven to hang out all day in a permanent state of leisure.

If those things are true, then this work thing we're assigned to do here on earth, this day job all of us seem forced to embrace to survive, that so many of us struggle through, tolerate, groan about, and count down the days until we can retire from, that thing must be a temporary consequence of something horrifically gone wrong.

A recent Gallup poll revealed that eighty-five percent of people hate their jobs. Everybody's working for the weekend. If work is so awful, then surely it must be a byproduct of the Fall. Work must have come about when sin came into the world.

No one ever taught me this, but it's what I fear many of us logically deduce from our own experience. It's Looney Tunes Theology.

FALSE NARRATIVES

We all have these internal narratives. They're called worldviews. They're the lenses through which we make sense of our everyday experience. Entire volumes have been written on this subject, so I will only touch on it briefly, but our worldviews are both learned and absorbed. They come from our families and our surrounding culture, from intentional teaching, and sometimes from good ol' Saturday morning cartoons.

The way we see our daily work is part of that human experience, so this internal storyline—our worldview—plays a huge role in crafting how we see and feel about the jobs we head out to each morning when the alarm clock goes off.

The origin and ending of a secular worldview bookend a finite lifespan. In this worldview, this world is all there is, so men and women are driven to reap all the happiness they can from the few years of life they have here on earth. Since there is no higher calling to which to submit, it is winner take all. Work is a means to power, comfort, and pleasure. Get yours while you can.

Even the modern Christian worldview has embraced portions of this false narrative. We've truncated the holistic message of the Kingdom and clouded the eternal significance of our human vocation here on this earth. We may get our origin story right, but our ending vision is often more Gnostic than gospel.

Many Christians believe that "spiritual work" (pastor, missionary, church employee) is the highest form of work here on this earth, so the main purpose of work for those who find themselves in "second tier secular jobs" is to make as much money as possible so they can financially support those doing the real spiritual work. That's really the extent of it. Endure, give, maybe volunteer to help in the nursery on Sunday, and hang on for that halo, harp, and cloud in eternity.

I'm oversimplifying to make a point, but if our ultimate hope is to be evacuated from this dying world into some kind of disembodied afterlife in the clouds, then the years we spend here on earth are just about biding our time until Jesus returns, and we can finally start on the spiritual part of our existence that really matters.

If that's the case, then our day jobs are more about making the most of this temporary season of "triage" here in this temporal world and only have a financial connection to our faith. Some of us are more fortunate and land great gigs that we love while some of us have to struggle more in work that we hate. But hey, all of it just burns up one day anyway, so it doesn't really matter, right? Survive and advance.

I truly believe this incomplete gospel narrative has locked many Christ followers into a sense of vocational purposelessness today.

THE REAL STORY?

What does the Great Story we explored in the last chapter really tell us about the origins and endings of our everyday work? How do our individual narratives fit within that great narrative and ignite a renewed purpose for our day jobs? Here are a few theological truths about your faith and your work that might just blow your mind:

In the beginning there was work.

In the beginning, at the genesis of the universe, at the origin of mankind and the earth itself, there was work. Work has always been an intentional facet of God's original design for you and me. This blew my mind. Let's go all the way back to Genesis and unpack the origins of this a little:

> *Thus the heavens and the earth were finished, and all the host of them. And on the seventh day God finished his* **work** **that he had done,** *and he rested on the seventh day from all his* **work that he had done.** *So God blessed the seventh day and made it holy, because on it God rested from all his* **work that he had done** *in creation.* (Genesis 2:1–3, emphasis mine)

Are you sensing a pattern here?

> *The* Lord *God took the man and put him in the garden of Eden* **to work it and keep it.** *(Genesis 2:15, emphasis mine)*

You don't have to be a brilliant theologian to note that we are just in Genesis 2. The whole tree and the serpent and the fruit and the fall of man doesn't happen until Chapter 3. Work is not some post-Fall punishment for our sin; rather, it's part of God's original design for mankind!

Yes, like everything else here in the "shadowlands,"[7] we experience our work through the curse of sin on the world. "Thorns and thistles" have become part of our working reality in this life (Genesis 3:18). But while work is under the curse, work is not the curse. As part of God's original design, it has a redemption story, too.

"When we work, we reflect God's image."

Regardless of what our Looney Tunes Theology taught us, we weren't created to sit on clouds and play harps all day. That's not where we came from and that's not where we're going. We were made to dream and build and serve and cultivate, to problem solve, to make culture, and to add value to the world around us. We were made to "work and keep" God's creation. This is the human vocation!

We were created to work. In the beginning there was work. This is foundational to your theological understanding of your day job.

When we work, we reflect God's image.

While the opening chapters of Genesis reveal to us a God who works, they also reveal something key about you and me: We were made in God's image.

---

7   Another C. S. Lewis reference, from *The Last Battle*: "'There was a real railway accident,' said Aslan softly. 'Your father and mother and all of you are—as you used to call it in the Shadowlands—dead. The term is over: the holidays have begun. The dream is over: this is the morning.'"

*Then God said, "Let us **make man in our image,** after our likeness. And let them have **dominion** over the fish of the sea and over the birds of the heavens and over the livestock and over all the earth and over every creeping thing that creeps on the earth." So God created man **in his own image, in the image of God** he created him; male and female he created them. (Genesis 1:26–27, emphasis mine)*

The Latin phrase for image of God is *imago Dei*. You and I were created in God's image. Modern culture has tried to reverse those roles, but it doesn't work that way. We didn't make God, God made us. Mankind is unique among all of God's creation. We are carriers of the very DNA of God Almighty.

And God is a *working* God.

You might say, "Yeah sure, but if God had a day job like me, surely He would be a brain surgeon, a billionaire manufacturer of sustainable clean energy, or a NASA rocket scientist. He did speak the whole cosmos into existence after all. What could this *imago Dei* thing possibly have to do with my kind of work?"

I love this quote by Tim Keller: "The current economic era has given us fresh impulses and new ways to stigmatize work such as farming and caring for children—jobs that are supposedly not 'knowledge' jobs and therefore do not pay very well. But in Genesis we see God as a gardener, and in the New Testament, we see him as a carpenter. No task is too small a vessel to hold the immense dignity of work given by God."[8]

Regardless of pay scale, educational requirements, or social hierarchy, all work has dignity and meaning and reflects the *imago Dei* in each one of us. When we work, we reflect God's image.

Our work is a partnership with God.

Let's stay in the first chapters of Genesis a little while longer.

> *And God blessed them. And God said to them, "Be fruitful and multiply and fill the earth and **subdue** it, and have **dominion** over the fish of the sea and over the birds of the heavens and over every living thing that moves on the earth." (Genesis 1:28, emphasis mine)*

Look at those two key concepts: Subdue. Have dominion.

Have you ever wondered why God didn't build houses, create neighborhoods, communities, cities, and cultures? Why did He stop with the raw materials?

Because creating with His creation is what we were created to do.

A vital part of our human vocation is to partner with God in the ongoing development of His world, to bring together the raw materials God has made and shape them, grow them, and develop them into something more. We partner with God as His vice-

---

8   Timothy Keller. *Every Good Endeavor.* New York City: Penguin Books, 2014. 49.

regents, as stewards who are acting on behalf of our King. We make culture and care for God's creation, including one another. From the simplest jobs to the most complex, our work is part of God's ongoing work in the world.

The father of the Protestant revolution, Martin Luther, said it most succinctly: "God is milking the cows through the vocation of the milkmaid."[9] There are not many milkmaids in the twenty-first century, but I could say it just as effectively using your work today, too:

- God is providing housing through the vocation of the property manager.
- God is educating children through the vocation of the teacher.
- God is feeding people through the vocation of the farmer.
- God is healing people through the vocation of the brain surgeon.
- God is raising children through the vocation of the stay-at-home-parent.
- God is keeping things ordered and sanitary through the vocation of the janitor.

How would it change your feelings about your job if you saw it like that?

9   Thomas Kepler. *The Table Talk of Martin Luther*. Mineola, NY: Dover Publications, 2005. 93–94.

Work is part of our heavenly future.

In Billy Graham's classic "My Answers" column that ran for decades in newspapers all over the United States, a reader lamented about a rumor he heard about work in heaven: "I used to think heaven was a place of rest, and I've always looked forward to going there. But recently I heard someone say that God has work for us to do in heaven. I'm having a hard time with this because I'm tired of working."

In his famous practical style, the evangelist replied with an encouraging clarification:

> *The Bible doesn't answer all our questions about heaven, but it certainly assures us that heaven will be a place of perfect peace and rest. The Bible says, "They will rest from their labor" (Revelation 14:13).*

> *At the same time, the Bible also says that God will have work for us in heaven—and we ought to be glad for this! After all, if all we did in heaven was sit around with nothing to do, we'd get very bored. But heaven won't be boring—and one reason is because God will have work for us to do. The Bible says, "His servants will serve him" (Revelation 22:3).*

> *But here is the amazing thing: In heaven, we'll never grow weary or tired, like we do here. When Adam and Eve rebelled against God, from that moment on work became a burden for the whole human race (see Genesis 3:17–19). But in heaven, that curse will be lifted, and work will no longer*

be a burden. Instead, it will be a joy! The Bible doesn't tell us exactly what it will be, but we'll be serving God—which is the highest honor imaginable.[10]

As we've already discovered, work was part of God's original design for mankind. Work was there at the beginning. It's not the work itself that is exhausting, meaningless, and overwhelming; it's sin's curse on our work that has broken its original place in God's created order.

Since you listened to your wife and ate from the tree whose fruit I commanded you not to eat, the ground is cursed because of you. All your life you will struggle to scratch a living from it. It will grow thorns and thistles for you, though you will eat of its grains. By the sweat of your brow will you have food to eat until you return to the ground from which you were made. (Genesis 3:17–19 NLT)

The new heaven and new earth will finally be free of these "thorns and thistles." The struggle, the sweat, and the curse will be permanently eradicated. Our work won't be gone, but it's sin-broken counterfeit will be. God's original intent for our lives and our work will finally be fully and completely restored. Work—redeemed and resurrected work—will most definitely be part of our heavenly future.

---

10   Billy Graham. "Our Work in Heaven Will Be a Joy, Not a Burden." Billy Graham Evangelistic Association, http://billygraham.org/answer/our-work-in-heaven-will-be-a-joy-not-a-burden/ (accessed April 19, 2021).

Until then, we are the foretaste of this glorious reality still to come. Through Christ, God's people can reach into that eternal future and pull a first taste of it back into the present, embracing our marketplace roles now as resurrected agents of God's kingdom in this season of the already but not yet.

– *Travel and Tourism* –

There's a deeply meaningful picture hanging on my office wall. Even as I write, it's in my peripheral vision just over the left corner of my computer screen. It's a beautiful artistic rendering of the first phrase of Psalm 23 in Arabic calligraphy: The Lord is my shepherd. I received it from a BAM missionary in 2016. He and his wife pioneered one of the first BAM projects The Stone Table ever funded, and their work has been wildly successful.

They live and work in a strategic city on the Arabian Peninsula, a coastal community where many indigenous people come to vacation. During the summer, you cannot turn around without bumping into a Saudi, Kuwaiti, or Qatari family. The area is also a political pressure-release valve. Because of its physical geography, the city is flooded with refugees escaping the surrounding war-torn countries. There are unreached people groups everywhere.

The ministry opportunities are vast, but these BAM missionaries needed a valid reason to live there to engage these people. A travel and tourism company became that platform. By serving the massive tourist market, these BAM missionaries provide a highly coveted service to the community, including steady jobs for multiple locals, and out-of-town cashflow to the economy. They're also building relationships, sharing Jesus, and planting a church through the business.

My favorite story from this project came through an email I received a few years after The Stone Table's initial investment. Not only was the proclamation of the gospel proving to be very profitable, so was the business itself. In their first two years of operations, the travel and tourism company had generated enough income to pay back all the seed money—they wanted to know where to send the check.

We reached out to their area leadership and learned about another BAM business they desired to start in the region. The profits from one business became the start-up funds for another. The seeds were multiplying, both economically and spiritually. This is business as mission at its finest.

CHAPTER

6

The Lord's Prayer for Marketplace Believers

I have so much to do that I shall spend the first three hours in prayer.

MARTIN LUTHER

I t's hard to pray, at least consistently, daily, and effectively. We can spout all the super-spiritual mantras about prayer that we want. We know it's vital to Christian living, the health of our daily relationships, our family, the impact of our work, our ability to lead. We know we *should* pray. We believe we should want to pray. But when it comes to the practical reality of *actually praying,* most of us find it frustrating, mysterious, and difficult.

It's much easier for most Christians to engage with Scripture than it is to pray with any kind of consistency, confidence, or authority.

I would dare say a majority of Christ followers carry the shame of underachieving in this lifeblood of the Christian faith.

If we want our little stories, our supporting cast subplots, to wrap themselves completely and fully into God's story, prayer is something we must get much more comfortable with. If we want our day jobs, our businesses, and our career paths to find fullness and meaning in this life, then the vital "work of prayer" has to become more integrated into our daily work.

Prayer is not some power I conjure up to magically get God to engage in my story. It's not the way that I guarantee a promotion or miraculously improve my business's bottom line. Prayer is about humbly aligning me with what God wants

"Prayer is essential to finding our work story within God's Great Story."

and is already at work doing, the story He is already telling. Prayer is essential to finding our work story within God's Great Story.

If prayer is an essential marketplace practice, how do marketplace believers get better at it? I hate doing things that make me feel dumb (this is a big reason I stay away from hardware stores). I want to know how to get *smarter* at praying.

Countless books have been written on the subject by authors much more versed in prayer than I am, but I hope this chapter can provide a practical guide for prayer within a daily work context. I stumbled upon a historic approach to Jesus' teaching on prayer that has helped me immeasurably over the last few years. It gives me a practical daily path to finding my story inside of God's story. Martin Luther and other church fathers used this as a simple gateway to effective prayer, and I think you will find it powerful in your life, too.

THE LORD'S MODEL PRAYER

Before "freeform" praying for his own needs or the pressing issues of the day, Luther would pray through the Lord's Prayer from Matthew 6, putting each phrase into his own words. I've found this process incredibly liberating. It gives me a clear biblical roadmap to express my own thoughts, hopes, and fears, and doesn't leave me stranded in the wilderness of my own wandering ideas and emotions.

Let's take a look at each of the six core phrases in the Lord's model prayer and see how they provide a simple pathway into the powerful discipline of prayer within our daily work context. If you want to find your story within God's Great Story, you need to start here.

1. Our Father in heaven, hallowed be your name (Matthew 6:9).

The first phrase of the Lord's Prayer is positional. It puts me in my rightful place and God in His.

First and foremost, it's relationally positional. We are part of a family. We have a Father. Perhaps that word conjures up bad images from your own upbringing, but I assure you God is the true and beautiful standard of fatherhood. He's what you always imagined a loving father to be. Father God is a trustworthy patriarch. He's our eternal identity source. We are image-bearers of our heavenly Father and carriers of His DNA.

While this phrase "our Father" displays our renewed relationship with God through Christ, it's not only relationally positional, but also morally positional. Our Father is holy, and He is *the* standard. This idea of God is not popular in today's post-modern culture, but it's vital for our flourishing as image-bearers of the Creator. Yes, God is love, but He is also holy! He is truth and love. We are under God's leadership both relationally *and* morally.

He is God. We are not. It's only under this relational and moral authority that we are able to function fully as human beings. We must declare this positional relationship and authority every day because we are prone to forget. If you want your work story to find its eternal meaning in Christ, it starts here.

Example:

Our Father in heaven, holy is Your name. Lord, I thank You today that You are my Father, that You are the perfect example of what fatherhood is intended to be. Thank you for making me in Your image. I trust myself to Your loving care and nurture today, but You are the One in charge. You are the standard bearer, and I look to You and not my own desires, not to my own narrative, not to the influence of the culture around me, but to You today as my holy and loving Father. Resurrect Your DNA in my life. May I honor Your name and Your position in and over me today. May the work of my hands, great or small, find its eternal meaning in and through You.

2. Your kingdom come, your will be done, on earth as it is in heaven (Matthew 6:10).

Here we submit to the sovereignty of God in our lives. Our families, our work, our communities, our nation, and everything in the world belong to Him. The word "kingdom" refers to God's dominion, His reign and rulership. As we outlined earlier, while Jesus' resurrection ushered in God's kingdom, His dominion over all creation is not yet fully on earth as it is in heaven.

We live in the overlap. Every aspect of our lives and our daily work exist in the "already but not yet," this middle act of God's Great Story. So, we experience both the firstfruit blessings of Christ's kingdom alongside the broken realities of this sinful world. We live in this tension, and so we pray for more of God's kingdom to reign in us and through us and through His people.

We also pray for God's will, His desires, plans, and purposes. I often find myself praying that God's will would swallow up my own. That down to a cellular level, God would resurrect my impulses and instincts so that they mirror His. I ask that He reorders the things I love to match the things He loves. This act of daily submission to the dominion and will of God is a vital and powerful part of daily prayer.

Example:

Your kingdom come, Your will be done, on earth as it is in heaven. Lord, today I ask that Your kingdom would take more dominion in my heart, in my family, in my work, and in the world around us. God, I don't trust my own heart. I'm not

*sure which desires to trust and which ones to be suspicious of,
so I give You all of them. I need You to come and reorder the
things that are important to me. Lord, I want to want what
You want today! Rewire me from the inside out, and where I
have not yet come into alignment with Your desires, give me
the grace to live in the tension. May Your purposes come to
bear in my life and in all my work today.*

3. Give us this day our daily bread (Matthew 6:11).

This segment of the Lord's Prayer is about daily returning to our
Source. Our power is not stored up in our knowledge, our job, our
source of income, our networks, our bank account, or our political
system. Our power as believers is in our ongoing dependence on
Jesus Christ.

Left to our own devices, we begin to trust in things other than
Jesus. Like food for our physical bodies, we must return to our
true Source for daily sustenance. The late Pastor Jack Miller,
author and pastor of New Life Presbyterian Church in Jenkintown,
Pennsylvania, phrased it this way: "We organize our lives and
plan our futures, and what lurks deep in our hearts is a desire for
security to replace our need for Jesus."

What happened to the manna in the wilderness when the Israelites
tried to store it up? It spoiled! God said, "I will feed you every
day; just trust Me." Yet His people tried to take His miraculous
provision and store it up so they didn't have to depend on Him
anymore. We do the exact same thing. We want to trust what
we can see, feel, touch, and control, but God knows we're only

living as we were created when He is the ongoing object of our dependence and trust. Our daily bread.

Example:

Give us this day our daily bread. Lord, I know my heart wants to find its rest in things I can control. I make idols, I store up treasure, I desperately try to create my own security. But today I return to You, the only true Source! I place my dependence in You, not my family, my job, my retirement account, my preferred political party. I place my dependence 100 percent on You fresh and new again today. Be my wisdom, be my strength, be my provider, be my daily bread for this day. Tomorrow I'll be back, again, because it's only in You that I place my trust.

4. Forgive us our debts, as we also have forgiven our debtors (Matthew 6:12).

God's grace is the lifeblood of our daily existence as Christians. My only hope for righteousness is to accept the gift of Jesus' righteousness freely offered to me. We humans are so screwed up by sin that even when we do good things, the silent motivation under those good deeds is often driven by self-righteousness and ulterior motives. Our daily work can easily slide into "works-righteousness," where we're no longer working from a place of Jesus-finished work, but in a vain attempt to forge our own identity and salvation.

We must return to grace. We must breathe grace. We must bathe in grace. We cannot fully live without the grace of Jesus alive and at work in us and through us every day.

It's not only our need for forgiveness that this phrase of the Lord's model prayer illuminates; it's also our need to forgive as well. Jesus starkly warns us just a couple verses later that if you don't forgive others, the Father won't forgive you (Matthew 6:15). It's much easier to realize our own need for grace than it is to offer that same grace to others. While reaching up to God with pleas for mercy with one hand, our other hand is often holding an offending brother in a chokehold. This cannot be.

This "forgiven forgiver" identity is one we must return to each day, especially as believers active in the marketplace. The grace of Jesus at work in our workplace through business transactions and relationships is the most potent daily declaration of the gospel we can make as marketplace Christians. This doesn't mean we stop holding people accountable or roll over and allow ourselves to be taken advantage of in a business deal, but it does mean we treat those across the negotiating table with the same grace we desperately need from Jesus.

I don't know what you've experienced. You may have extreme pain and brokenness in your past, things so dark and painful you don't know how to let go of them. If you can't find grace for others inside yourself, let God's grace to you overflow from your life into theirs, even those that have hurt you deeply.

Example:

Forgive us our debts as we forgive our debtors. Jesus, I come to You again as a humble sinner in need of grace. Sin is like a disease that is rooted in my flesh, and You are the only remedy. May I live and breathe Your grace today! May I live from Your forgiveness in my own life and may that grace empower me to holiness today in every aspect of my life, including my work. And for those I struggle to forgive, God, may Your grace to me overflow as grace through me. May I be a forgiven forgiver today.

5. Lead us not into temptation, but deliver us from evil (Matthew 6:13).

There is sin in me, and there is sin all around me. I need to pray for protection from both. Left to my own devices, I will migrate toward fulfilling the identity hole in my life through my own means. I will look to my idols, and in seeking to satisfy my own internal longings, I will be tempted to do some awful things. When I ask God to help me avoid temptation, I'm praying that the Creator would help me cast off my sin nature and resurrect my original design, the me I was always made to be in Him.

We need to pray for protection from the sin within us, but we also need to pray for protection from the sin all around us. We have an enemy seeking to steal, kill, and destroy (John 10:10). Pray for protection over families, spouses, children, businesses, communities, our countries, and the entire world. Pray for supernatural preservation over your business and the work of your hands, that the "locusts" won't devour your "crops." Pray that evil would have no foothold in your staff and co-workers. Pray that what the enemy intends for evil God would turn to good. Pray that God would rewrite every difficulty we face into the fulfillment of His Great Story.

Example:

Lead us not into temptation, but deliver us from evil. Left to my own devices today, Lord, I will succumb to sin. I will worship my idols. I will seek to fulfill my own identity in my own way, and it will break my relationship with You and others. Protect me from my own depravity, Lord! Protect me from this sin within me as well as the evil all around me; from those who would try to kill and destroy what You are resurrecting and renewing. Protect us from the evil one and his work in this world.

6. For Yours is the kingdom and the power and the glory forever. Amen (Matthew 9:13 NKJV).

The doxology—mostly recognized today by its climactic crescendo when the Lord's Prayer is set to music—was only found in certain fragments of the original Scripture. For that reason, most modern translations of the Bible no longer carry it. I always leave it in. It powerfully leaves us right where we started: glorifying the Great Story writer! The doxology refocuses my spirit on who God is and what my place is within His grand narrative.

There is this inherent imagery we cling to that tells us we are the central characters in our own story, but that's not how we were designed, nor is it how we flourish and find eternal meaning in this life. We were not created to be the main character in a story that we are writing about ourselves; rather, we were made to be beloved members of the supporting cast in a divine masterpiece that God has been writing since the beginning of time.

When we live as if we are the center of our story, as if our happiness, our desires, and our passions are central, we are actually living outside our created design and heading for ultimate misery. This doxology puts me back in my proper place and God fully in His. If you want to find renewed meaning in your daily work, finish your daily prayers with the doxology.

> *Example:*
>
> *For Yours is the Kingdom and the power and the glory! I declare today, Lord, that You at the center and I am on the periphery. You are at the center and I revolve around You! You are the main character in the story of this day, and I am here to serve the telling of Your story. Today is Yours, Lord. The dominion, power, and glory are Yours, Lord. I am Yours, today, Lord. Amen.*

THE POWER OF PRAYER

Do you see how this simple model can work as a bridge to prayer? It makes the ethereal mystery of prayer more accessible, and I think that was Jesus' intent. From this point, my prayers and petitions can flow in their own freeform manner because they have been shaped by Jesus' gateway.

Prayer is powerful because it forces our hearts into a place of humble submission and surrender, right where we were created to live and flourish in God Himself. The Lord's Prayer will completely transform the way you approach your daily work, no matter what that work is.

– *Soccer as Mission* –

As a diehard fan of the NFL, I love to make good-hearted jokes about soccer. Yes, I know soccer is the most popular sport globally and that I'm vastly outnumbered by a passionate and growing international fanbase, but it's fun to poke the bear from time to time (and all in good fun).

That said, soccer as mission (or in this case, football as mission) is no joke. In 2008, a retired European professional footballer was finding his second career as a successful businessman. He and his family had immigrated to the United States and were living the American dream: six-figure salary, big house, a seemingly limitless future.

But the Lord began to stir their hearts for those unreached with gospel. Shortly after, the family felt led to leave everything they thought they ever wanted to move to Southeast Asia as full-time missionaries. It didn't take long for them to feel their inadequacy. They were surrounded by incredibly gifted missionaries with theology degrees who were great at preaching. What did they possibly have to offer?

That's when our footballer friend clearly heard the Holy Spirit speak: "I've given you something. Now use it!" Those gifts were business and football.

In 2010, they started the first football academy in their community. The local army base quickly contracted the academy to teach their soldiers to play. The police department's football club followed soon after. Suddenly, these "inadequate missionaries" were surrounded by hundreds of football enthusiasts of all ages and backgrounds. Today, the academy boasts its own Astroturf soccer field, and indigenous leaders from the local community profitably run the day-to-day operations.

The natural comradery fostered by sports leads to genuine relationships and regular conversations about faith.

"Hey coach, can I stop by your house?"

"Hey coach, can you join us for dinner?"

"Hey coach, where can I get a copy of the Injil [Arabic New Testament]?"

This football academy has become one of the most successful BAM stories in the world, both financially and spiritually. They are currently expanding their model to another city in the north where they will gain access to thousands of new football enthusiasts from unreached people groups. These unlikely missionaries are building a business, employing locals, making Jesus famous, and planting the church among unreached people groups to the glory of God through soccer.

7

Reimagining Meaningful Work

Deprived of meaningful work, men and women lose their reason for existence; they go stark, raving mad.

FYODOR DOSTOEVSKY

There has been growing pushback against the pornography industry in recent months. A major porn website was recently shutdown because authorities discovered two-thirds of their content was grossly illegal (for reasons I will not expound on for our purposes here). I bring this up, not to discuss the vile hijacking of God's beautiful design for sex, but because of some disturbing online commentary I noticed that the news triggered.

In response to one story about how sex work is destroying lives, one guy responded: "All work is prostitution. You're just commodifying yourself to the highest bidder."

Another replied: "Self-debasement for profit. Nothing noble or respectable about it. You just described all work."

In the risk of assuming social media opinion is a reflection of the majority, I've seen growing efforts to try and classify all work as a form of abuse and something we should strive to do away with completely as society progresses.

These are disturbing perspectives and show a complete misunderstanding of the eternal nature and divine purposes for work. As someone who has visited Project Rescue[11] homes filled with victims of the sex trafficking industry, I know a few hundred women and children who would be deeply offended by the ridiculous comparison of normal everyday jobs and forced prostitution.

MEANINGLESS WORK

We were designed for meaningful work, and as Christians we need to reclaim that meaning from a culture that seems to have fallen into an Ecclesiastes moment:

> *"Meaningless! Meaningless!" says the Teacher. "Utterly meaningless! Everything is meaningless." (Ecclesiastes 1:2 NIV)*

---

11   Project Rescue exists "to rescue and restore victims of sexual slavery through the love of and power of God." Learn more at www.projectrescue.com.

There are many reasons for this current cultural temperament. For one, most of us are looking for something from our jobs that our jobs simply cannot provide (keep reading; get to Part 2). But further, most of us have simply lost sight of this bigger storyline in which our day jobs are set. We struggle to find meaning because we lost the spiritual connection between balancing a general ledger, waiting a table, fixing a leaky faucet, or sweeping a floor and the Great Story of God and His work in the world.

As Tim Keller eloquently puts it: "Our work can be a calling only if it is reimagined as a mission of service to something beyond merely our own interests. Thinking of work mainly as a means of self-fulfillment and self-realization slowly crushes a person and undermines society itself."[12]

Some vocations, like doctors, teachers, or pastors, are much closer to the direct impact of their work than others. The greater the distance between your work and your ability to see the mission of service that it creates, the easier it is to become disillusioned.

THE SACRED WORK OF CLEANING UP THE TRASH

Some jobs are celebrated, while others are merely tolerated. Which job holds more prestige: the brain surgeon or the local fast-food restaurant employee? What if all "classes" of work, all fields of work hold sacred and meaningful value?

---

12   Timothy Keller. *Every Good Endeavor.* New York City: Penguin Books, 2014.

I love this quote from Amy Sherman: "Every faithful act of service, every honest labor to make the world a better place, which seemed to have been forever lost and forgotten in the rubble of history, will be seen on that day [at the final resurrection] to have contributed to the perfect fellowship of God's kingdom.... All who committed their work in faithfulness to God will be by Him raised up to share in the new age, and will find that their labor was not lost, but that it has found its place in the completed."[13]

In Christ, there is no such thing as meaningless work; it's all meaningful.

Last year I had a beautiful and unexpected encounter on a long trip home that deeply impacted my perspective on this issue. I was flying from Los Angeles to Indianapolis via Atlanta after meeting with potential investors in our housing company. When you lose three hours on an already long, cross-country flight, it makes for an extremely late night.

My colleagues and I were sitting at Gate B27 in a mostly empty Atlanta airport, watching the last few minutes of a West Coast NBA game on one of the terminal television screens. As a major hub for many airlines, Atlanta is almost always packed with travelers. The sparse corridors and darkened food courts were a reminder of the late hour.

---

13   Amy Sherman. *Kingdom Calling: Vocational Stewardship for the Common Good.* Downers Grove, IL: IVP Books, 2011.

As we waited for our 11 p.m. connecting flight to Indy at a mostly empty gate, a young girl with a broom, dustpan, and trash cart began sweeping under the seats around us. I could hear her singing quietly to herself as she approached. Without even looking up, I could feel her bubbly energy.

"Are we in your way?" I asked, as she filled her rolling bin with a day's worth of trash from thousands of hurried travelers. "We're happy to get up and move to some other seats so you can sweep more easily under this section of chairs."

"Absolutely not!" she energetically replied with a grin. "You just sit right there and relax. I'll take care of this. Don't you worry yourself."

Her extremely pleasant demeanor caught me off guard a bit. As a morning person, my brain had already initiated its shutdown mode by this time of night. But her personality was still magnetic, and she stopped sweeping long enough to engage me in conversation.

"Where are you guys heading tonight?" she asked.

I told her we'd been in California for a business meeting and were catching the last flight of the night to get home to family.

It turns out that her day had been an adventure, too. She found someone's lost luggage while she was cleaning. It was a carry-on bag that looked like it had some important, personal things in it. She was concerned that just taking it to the lost and found might cause a long delay in returning it to the owner, so she googled the name on the bag tag, somehow found a contact phone number, and called the person directly to let them know she found it and would make sure it was returned safely.

"I just couldn't rest until I made sure that man got his stuff back!" she touted with the good kind of pride.

"There are no small jobs when we do them unto the Lord."

She was such a breath of fresh air after a day of flying. Our interaction literally felt divine. As she pushed her cart out of view toward the next gate, I felt the Lord drop something in my heart that she needed to hear. I got up and ran down the terminal to catch up with her.

I startled her a bit (how would you feel if some crazy guy was running down an airport corridor chasing you?), but I had something I knew I needed to say. After I assured her that I wasn't a serial killer, I took a second to catch my breath.

"Thank you for what you do here," I told her. "There are no small jobs when we do them unto the Lord. Whether you realize it or not, you partnered with God tonight in caring for us and all these other weary passengers waiting for our planes. Your work matters. Thank you."

She seemed both grateful and stunned, as if she had never thought about her job that way before. But it was true. In that moment, she was God's business partner, doing His work in caring deeply for each one of us. She brought a little more life and beauty to an airplane terminal.

I want to do better in recognizing the sacredness of work, the meaningfulness of work, no matter how important or unimportant our culture may have deemed it to be. From the pilot who flew my plane to the young lady who swept under my seat at Gate B27, all work matters when viewed through the lens of honoring God and caring for people (i.e., the Great Commandment, coming up next).

What if we all saw our work and the work of those around us in that way?

REIMAGINE YOUR STORY

I graduated high school with a passion for music and a desire to break into the contemporary Christian music (CCM) industry in Nashville, Tennessee. I was an above-average keyboard player and a local standout (in my own mind and church community, at least).

After a friend got me backstage passes to a Michael W. Smith concert in Indy, I had a long conversation with the keyboard player in the band. He recommended a small school called Belmont in the heart of Nashville. I was hooked and I was in.

I moved to Nashville in 1992 with the shared aspirations of so many other young musicians. I wanted to work in the music industry. I wanted to be on stage. I wanted to go on tour with my CCM heroes. Maybe one day I would even have an album of my own!

I dreamed of stadium gigs with big time artists. What I landed was mailroom gig in the basement of Word Records.

Three days a week, I drove down to Music Row, walked through the same doors as all my favorite CCM artists, meandered down a long corridor lined with countless gold record displays, and caught the elevator to the windowless cavern buried beneath six floors of executive office suites.

It didn't have quite the comedic buzz of the basement mailroom in Will Ferrell's Christmas classic *Elf*, but mailrooms are mailrooms. For hours on end, my supervisor and I would meticulously sort each envelope by type, recipient, and floor, pull out the hundreds of unsolicited demo cassettes, wrap the related pieces in rubber bands, and load them onto push carts for delivery.

It was a great gig for a 19 year old, but I had a hard time connecting fingerfuls of paper cuts with working in the music business. I grew to resent the work, partly because I was immature and entitled, but mostly I think because it was so far removed from the ultimate impact of the work itself. I couldn't see how shuffling envelopes had anything to do with the awesome music I was passionate about. But it did.

By our culture's self-obsessed storyline, I was a "slave to the man." I was a "prostitute" to the powers that be. I was commodifying myself to the highest bidder. But through a gospel perspective, by sorting and delivering the mail I was actually partnering with God in His ongoing work in the world. I was taking disorder and making it orderly. I was taking chaos and making it functional. I was "working and keeping" part of God's creation. I was playing a beloved supporting cast role in God's Great Story.

This is more than just mind games and optimistic thinking. It's forcibly taking back the small, temporal human narrative this fallen world is selling and reimagining the work of our hands, great or small, through God's original design. It's making the meaningless meaningful.

As we continue, we will look more closely at the ways the gospel reshapes our everyday marketplace work into a daily opportunity to glorify God, love our neighbor, and proclaim the name of Jesus to the ends of the earth.

– *Rickshaws for Freedom* –

One of the most powerful redemption stories of the 2020 COVID-19 pandemic came out of Southeast Asia. While lockdowns restricted and isolated almost everyone in the world, the virus actually became a ticket to freedom for hundreds of women imprisoned in the vile sex-trafficking industry.

For the first time in centuries, brothels in various cities across Southern Asia were forcibly closed. The traffickers lost their entire revenue stream but were still faced with all the expenses associated with feeding and housing the women and children they enslaved. The economic pinch triggered something completely unheard of and totally unexpected. The traffickers began releasing hundreds of women; they even came to friends at Project Rescue and *asked for help.* "If you will take them, they are free to go," the traffickers told Project Rescue.

These trafficked women are enslaved in psychological shackles, convinced they owe huge debts to the traffickers. They are threatened that any effort to escape will be met with violence against their children and their families back home. And yet almost overnight, the traffickers threw open the prison doors and insisted the women leave! Only God can coordinate a liberation moment like this.

Hundreds of women and children immediately needed food, shelter, healthcare, and most importantly, a new way to support themselves. Project Rescue mobilized job training and micro-business development so that these women would no longer need the sex industry as their means to survive.

Auto-rickshaws are a large part of the transportation infrastructure in the large cities of Southeast Asia, but travel by auto-rickshaw can be very dangerous for women. Project Rescue raised funds to purchase and deploy a fleet of female-friendly auto-rickshaws equipped with panic buttons and emergency communication devices. Now women rescued from forced prostitution drive these widely used vehicles, leveraging the marketplace to not only meet a transportation need in the local community, but to also demonstrate the love of Jesus in a tangible way. The marketplace belongs to Jesus. The gospel really does redeem and resurrect *all* things.

.

II

Work and the Great Commandment

"Teacher, which is the great commandment in the Law?" And he said to him, "You shall love the Lord your God with all your heart and with all your soul and with all your mind. This is the great and first commandment. And a second is like it: You shall love your neighbor as yourself. On these two commandments depend all the Law and the Prophets."'

MATTHEW 22:36-40

CHAPTER

8

A Renewed Purpose for Work

Whatever your heart clings to and confides in,
that is really your God, your functional savior.

MARTIN LUTHER

The people of Israel in the Old Testament were a strangely fickle bunch. When I read their story through my modern, enlightened framework, I find it a bit perplexing.

After four hundred years in Egyptian slavery under the harsh leadership of Pharaoh, God showed up in spectacular fashion to set His special people free.

There were plagues of locusts and frogs. There were swarms of gnats and flies.

The Nile River turned to blood like a scene from some horror film.

And ultimately, the firstborn of every family whose door was not covered by the blood of the covenant lamb died during the night of Passover (Exodus 7–12).

If that wasn't enough…

After Pharaoh finally relented and let the Israelites go, there was a whole new set of jaw-dropping miracles.

The breath of God split the Red Sea in two so His fleeing people could cross to the other side completely on dry land (Exodus 14).

God Himself physically led His wandering children through the wilderness by manifesting His presence in a towering pillar of cloud by day and fire by night (Exodus 13). When it moved, they moved. When it stopped, they stopped. That's way more epic than my iPhone turn-by-turn navigation.

He provided breakfast, lunch, and dinner on the ground outside their tents every morning in the form of manna (which I like to think of as early-recipe Chick-fil-A nuggets). When they needed water, it spouted from a rock. When they craved meat, He sent more quail than they could possibly consume.

The people of Israel tangibly interacted with the miraculous, living presence of God every moment of the day.

And yet, as soon as God called their leader Moses up Mt. Sinai to receive the Ten Commandments, at the moment they were left on their own, they pooled their gold jewelry, melted it down, forged a golden statue in the shape of a cow, bowed down, and began worshipping it (Exodus 32).

These people are absolute morons! How blind and short-sighted could someone possibly be?! While the living God was visibly active and working in their midst, they still managed to lose sight of Him and traded-in the Creator of the universe for a self-made golden counterfeit. What a bunch of idiots.

It's funny how arrogant and condescending we can become when we watch others make a complete disaster of their lives. Permit me to remind you of a little something...

You and I do the exact same thing.

We make idols.

A majority of us don't actually have golden statues in the backyard that we bow down and worship every day. I mean, that's just asking for a nasty letter from the homeowners association. But we do have things we put in God's place. We do it instinctively, instantaneously, and incessantly.

WORK IDOLATRY

If we really want to understand idolatry, we need to think deeper than gold figurines. Because an idol is much more insidious than that.

An idol is anything we place our trust in, anything we try to find our identity in outside of God Himself. Idols are God-replacements, and removing God from His rightful place is the starting point of everything that is wrong in us and this fallen world.

Our modern minds tend to define sin by its broken outflow—by bad behavior. But the root of human sin is not "doing bad things," the root of all sin is actually idolatry. It's wrong worship. It's elevating something—anything, even good things—above God's ultimate place in our lives and in this world. Idolatry is our manic search to find ourselves in anything and everything except our Creator.

I can attest to this battle in my own life each and every day. I bet you can, too.

Our work can easily become one of these idols. We place our trust in our paycheck. We find our identity in the social status of our jobs. We define ourselves by what we do. Just like the Israelites dancing around that golden calf at the foot of Mt. Sinai, we replace the Creator with something we created. We manufacture eternal value in temporal things, and then we worship them.

The work itself is good, but what we try to make of it becomes problematic. We worship the work *instead of* worshipping God through our work. One of the reasons so many people struggle to find meaning and purpose in their day jobs is that they're trying to secure something through their work that it's ultimately incapable of providing them.

But the gospel changes all of that. And it starts with two simple words that we often get mixed up.

FOR VS. FROM

It's fascinating to watch these talent reality shows. Every week it seems at least one contestant bursts into tears after a great performance. Amidst the cheers of the crowd and accolades of the judges, the performer's sentiments usually sound something like: "I've worked so hard. It's so good to finally be seen, to be recognized, to be celebrated for what I can do. This just means so much!"

This is the default setting of the human heart: If I perform well, I will be loved, I will discover who I am, and I will finally matter. This inside drive doesn't only emerge on the stage of reality talent shows; it permeates our daily work as well. If I work hard, if I perform well, if I'm successful, then I will be valued by my colleagues, esteemed by my friends, and maybe God will finally be pleased with me, too.

Of course, we are called to work hard and do our jobs well. It's the right idea. Just in the wrong order.

We've unpacked that work was part of God's original design (Genesis 2). It's one of the ways we reflect His image and partner with Him in His ongoing work in the world (Genesis 1). Scripture clearly tells us to work hard (Ecclesiastes 9:10); that if you're lazy, you don't eat (2 Thessalonians 3:10); and that hard work creates profit (Proverbs 14:23).

But like anything in this life, our sin corrupts even the purest of motives. Left to our natural instincts, work becomes a means instead of a response. The mistake lies in confusing two similar sounding prepositions: for and from.

When I work *for,* I reject the gospel. I leverage my work to create my own identity. I trust in my effort to earn my own way. I perform *for* my worth. I make myself the hero of my story. In a sense I become my own savior, a role I am woefully incapable of playing. When we work *for* the approval of God and those around us, the true power of the grace-driven gospel is completely neutralized in our lives.

I love how Eugene Peterson paraphrased this in The Message Bible:

> *Let me put this question to you: How did your new life begin? Was it by working your heads off to please God? Or was it by responding to God's Message to you? Are you going to continue this craziness? For only crazy people would think they could complete by their own efforts what was begun by God. If you weren't smart enough or strong enough to begin it, how do you suppose you could perfect it? Did you go through this whole painful learning process for nothing? It is not yet a total loss, but it certainly will be if you keep this up!* (Galatians 3:2–4)

But when I get my prepositions correct, when I get the order right, when I swap *for* with *from,* my work actually becomes superpowered by the gospel. Let's learn some Greek.

MY FAVORITE WORD

When Jesus died on the cross, He said, "It is finished!" (John 19:30). The Greek word here is *tetelestai*. It's a business term often stamped on first century receipts that literally means "paid in full."

I have this word framed and hanging over the desk in my office. I also wear it on a brown rubber bracelet on my wrist. I never want to forget that Jesus' finished work is the foundation, the starting place, of all my work.

> *"Only when you rest in Jesus can your work find its true power and purpose."*

All those things you're working for—money, security, identity, worth, power, control, hope, peace—all of those things are found fully and only in Jesus Christ and His finished work for you. Only when you rest in Jesus can your work find its true power and purpose.

A healthy work ethic is beautiful when it's not fed by a root of self-righteousness. Grace is not a celebration of laziness. Grace does not negate the value of hard work. But grace does swap out the preposition. It's *from*, not for. We work *from* the place of "it is finished!" *Tetelestai.*

Which changes everything.

When I root my trust and my identity where it truly belongs, in Jesus Christ alone, then my everyday work can finally be freed to

Missional Marketplace

become what it was always designed to be: the fulfillment of the Great Commandment.

WORK AND THE GREAT COMMANDMENT

The religious leaders and power brokers of Jesus' day were often trying to trap Him into saying something controversial. In one of these encounters, a legal expert asked him to rank the Old Testament law, to go on record as to which of God's commandments was really the most important.

Jesus said all the laws and commandments could be summed up in Deuteronomy 6:5:

> *Jesus replied: "Love the Lord your God with all your heart and with all your soul and with all your mind." This is the first and greatest commandment. And the second is like it: "Love your neighbor as yourself." (Matthew 22:37–39 NIV)*

When work is my idol, when my career is my identity and how I ultimately define who I am, then my work becomes the foundation of my worth, my value, my acceptance, my status, my pride (or maybe even my shame). My work was not designed to carry this weight and responsibility.

But when my identity is firmly rooted in Jesus Christ, then my identity, my worth, and my status are permanently grounded in the resurrection life of the gospel. Who I am is settled because Jesus already settled it. Now my work, no matter how celebrated or menial, can finally become what God always designed it to be:

Worship to God and love to my neighbor—the fulfillment of the Great Commandment.

Every day when our alarms go off, you and I have a brand-new opportunity to honor God and love people through our work. It doesn't matter what that job might be, whether you're a lawyer or you serve coffee at the local cafe, all work is an opportunity to engage the Kingdom in this simple and profound way.

Unless you're involved in some kind of illegal criminal activity, the same can be said of any business, job, or role, great or small. If you want renewed meaning in your day job, reimagine it through the lens of the Great Commandment. Your work is a daily opportunity to engage in two activities Jesus said were of utmost priority: Loving God. Loving your neighbor.

We get the opportunity every day to worship God and love people through the work of our hands. There's a renewed purpose and meaning waiting for those who get up and go to work that way each day.

– *Marketing as Missions* –

A Romanian marketing company called Agency Boon (agencyboon.com) hosts The Stone Table's website. They are absolutely fabulous to work with, but their story goes much deeper than just providing high quality digital marketing services.

I met the founder when he was a youth pastor at a local church on the west side of Indianapolis. Ryan Crozier has a contagious personality, and his passion for Jesus, entrepreneurship, *and* the country of Romania couldn't be contained for long.

Before he set his sights cross-culturally, one of Ryan's first business start-up efforts was a pedicab company in downtown Indianapolis. Although the business didn't last long, it whet Ryan's appetite for entrepreneurship. It also began to illuminate a pathway toward an undeniable call to Romania he had felt since his teenage years.

Ryan and his wife moved to Bucharest with a deep desire to engage Romania with the gospel. In a post-Christian culture that sees little connection between religion and everyday life, Ryan began to utilize the marketplace, both nonprofit and for-profit, as an avenue to affect justice issues like human trafficking and sexual exploitation. These efforts got the attention of local authorities, and Ryan now has a value-add inroad to demonstrate and proclaim the gospel to the people God called him to reach decades ago.

Ryan's three organizations—Agency Boon, The Good Bureau, and eLiberare—employ local Romanians and provide high-quality services, not only to The Stone Table, but to other high-capacity, well-known businesses and ministries around the world.

Ryan leverages the marketplace, both as a platform for his family's presence in Romania and as a mechanism for bringing gospel life into the culture God burdened him for when he was a teenager. This is the holistic gospel coming to life through a Great Commission entrepreneur.

CHAPTER

9

Work, Worship, Service

We can do little things for God; I turn the
cake that is frying on the pan for love of him,
and that done, if there is nothing else to call
me, I prostrate myself in worship before him,
who has given me grace to work; afterwards
I rise happier than a king.

BROTHER LAWRENCE

M y career path looks a bit like a drunkard's walk. I started out as a piano major in college, graduated with a degree in accounting, and started as an auditor for a CPA firm. Five years later, I became a music pastor and eventually a church planter, spending a dozen years in full-time vocational ministry. Now, I find myself back in the marketplace, leading a real estate nonprofit that gives half its profits to global missions. It's not a path any career counselor could plot, but God has certainly used all of it.

My first grown-up job was at a CPA firm in Indianapolis. As far as accounting firms go, it was pretty family friendly. My wife and I were newly married and just starting to forge our way in the world, and public accounting experience was highly recommended by all my professors and advisers.

There was only one problem—I hated accounting. You'd think I would have discovered this earlier, but my good grades might have masked my disdain for the subject matter.

My first full year at the firm I was assigned to an inventory count for a large manufacturing company in northern Indiana. Auditors try to complete these counts as close to the end of the year as possible, so this job landed me on a scissor lift in a cold warehouse on Christmas Eve. While suspended thirty feet in the air, I took a widget from a cardboard box, shivered from the cold, added a tick mark to my count sheet, blew on my frozen hands, placed the widget in a second box, and repeated the exercise for hours on end until the sample size was done.

All I could think about while repeating this tedious and seemingly never-ending process was, "What sin could I have possibly committed to deserve this cosmic punishment?!" There was no way you could've convinced me that this job was sacred, that it had any eternal meaning. If it wasn't so cold, I would've believed I was toiling in the very pit of hell itself. Surely it was sin that brought this horrific thing called work into the world, and one glorious day in heaven work would be cast into the lake of fire with the devil and all his minions, and there would be much rejoicing. (Twenty-three year olds can be a bit dramatic at times; maybe you've noticed.)

Of course, this understanding of our day jobs certainly isn't true. I wish someone could have helped me see the bigger gospel-infused picture.

FILL IN THE BLANK

Statistics say a majority of people hate their jobs. A few of us are lucky enough to be passionate about our work, but most of us tolerate work as something that "just has to be done." After all, there are bills to pay, kids to feed, loans to pay off, and maybe if we're lucky, a few extra dollars leftover to do something fun from time to time. That was certainly true of my first job out of college.

This is just the reality of life, right? The rat race. It's days of mostly uninspiring obligation sprinkled with a few occasional glimpses of happiness here and there.

Work is boring. Work is hard. Work is meaningless.

Or perhaps you find yourself in the opposite camp. You're one of the lucky ones whose work makes you feel good about your place in the social hierarchy. Maybe it pays you big dollars and the money gives you the ability to silence many of the fears and insecurities that others hear more loudly in life.

Work is status. Work is identity. Work is power.

How about you? How would you finish that sentence?

Work is _____.

Have you ever wondered how God might fill in that blank?

When you read Genesis 2:15 and discover that God made us to "work and keep" His creation, what do you imagine He had in mind? If we dig into the deeper meaning of the Old Testament Hebrew word for work, it actually gives us a powerful clue as the ancient Hebrew language is rich with meaning. Modern English doesn't always do justice to the deep and colorful nuances that can be pulled from Old Testament linguistic origins. The original Hebrew gives us a more holistic understanding of this thing we call work. The Hebrew word for work in the Old Testament is *avodah*. *Avodah* paints a beautiful word picture of God's rich meaning for everyday work lives.

WORK AS WORK

In Psalm 104, *avodah* means work as we naturally understand it in the modern world:

> *Man goes out to his work [avodah] and to his labor until the evening. (Psalm 104:23)*

This is our traditional understanding of work. The alarm goes off in the morning. We hit snooze (six or seven times). We get up, make our coffee, get cleaned up, and head out to the office. We go to work, to our *avodah*.

In this instance, *avodah* means our day jobs. *Avodah* is what we do for a living. But *avodah* is so much deeper than that.

WORK AS WORSHIP

In Exodus 8, this same exact word seems to mean something completely different:

> Then the LORD said to Moses, "Go to Pharaoh and say to him, 'This is what the LORD says: Let my people go, so that they may worship [avodah] me.'" (*Exodus 8:1 NIV*)

When Moses confronted Pharaoh, he was about to lead the Israelites from their captivity in Egypt so that they could go and worship God in the wilderness. This word for worship is also *avodah*, the same word in Psalm 104 that means traditional work.

Avodah is work and *avodah* is worship.

WORK AS SERVICE

In Joshua 24, this same word has yet another rich layer to it:

> But as for me and my household, we will serve [avodah] the LORD. (*Joshua 24:15 NIV*)

My mom had this verse prominently displayed in a picture frame in the hallway of our home when I was a kid. We will serve, we will *avodah* the Lord.

The Hebrew word for work is the exact same word for worship and service.

ADDING VALUE

There is a false caricature today that the marketplace, and in turn our work in it, is primarily about extracting value from others solely for personal benefit. Popular culture loves to portray the businessman as the power-hungry villain, and sin has certainly given us plenty of broken counterfeits of the true God-honoring design for marketplace work. But all work (*avodah*) is first and foremost about worshipping (*avodah*) God and serving (*avodah*) our neighbor. When we go to work, we add value to other people's lives and the community around us.

For those redeemed by the gospel, work is not how we forge an identity for ourselves, nor is it some horrific punishment for sin. Work is *work*, work is *worship*, and work is *service*. Work is the way we provide for our families while giving glory to God and loving our fellow man.

Sound familiar? *Avodah* is ultimately the fulfillment of the Great Commandment. Love God and love your neighbor. Let's take a closer look at this neighbor part.

YOUR NEIGHBOR = THE ECONOMY

There's a scene in the iconic Frank Capra classic *It's a Wonderful Life* in which George Bailey fights off a run on the Bailey Building and Loan. In the chaos that ensues, Bailey successfully talks down a lobby full of panicked customers demanding the immediate withdrawal of their cash by helping them understand one vital aspect of basic economics.

He passionately explains that the Building and Loan is not an independent entity in and of itself; it's actually the interdependent connection of everyone in the community. Here's how the dialog unfolded: "You're thinking of this place all wrong. As if I had the money back in a safe. The money's not here. Your money's in Joe's house...right next to yours, and in the Kennedy house, and Mrs. Macklin's house, and a hundred others. Why, you're lending them the money to build, and then, they're going to pay it back to you as best they can. Now what are you going to do, foreclose on them? ...Now wait...now listen...now listen to me. I beg of you not to do this thing."[14]

Now, I'll try my best George Bailey impersonation here and tie this illustration to the way believers in Jesus understand the vital human aspects of their daily work. Perhaps nothing shined a light on this fundamental misunderstanding more clearly than the coronavirus pandemic of 2020.

---

14   *It's a Wonderful Life*. Directed by Frank Capra. Los Angeles: RKO Radio Pictures, 1946.

During the understandable chaos that ensued, I watched well-meaning (and sometimes well-educated) people prove their ignorance of fundamental economic concepts. I heard a lot of phrases thrown around like:

- We've just temporarily shut down "the economy."
- We need to reopen "the economy."
- Don't you care about people? All you talk about is "the economy."

Through a few phrases, we turned the marketplace into a lifeless entity. Like the panicked patrons of the Bailey Building and Loan, we imagined we could somehow separate "the economy" from our neighbor. But the economy is not some inanimate object that exists in and of itself, the economy *is* people. In its simplest form, the economy is the intertwining of human lives in mutual service to one another.

A POWDER KEG CONVERSATION

I waded into this discussion to my own peril. In a short Facebook post, I tried to convey the very human and sacred nature of *the economy* as a backdrop to this horrific coronavirus outbreak. It was greeted with both cheers and disdain (which seems to be the binary tradition of our modern world). Some thanked me for saying it, while others accused me of idolizing capitalism and hating the elderly.

I normally try to keep my social media presence controversy-free, but COVID-19 definitely changed the rules. Our sweet spot at The Stone Table is the intersection of the marketplace and God's mission in the world, so when the global economy effectively goes on hiatus, when entrepreneur friends start losing their businesses and countless employees are furloughed and sent to the unemployment office, we felt compelled to engage with it through the lens of the gospel.

For all those who already feel their blood beginning to boil, I will reiterate a few things we've already explored in this book:

- Work, business, and the marketplace were all part of God's original design; however, broken by sin, they do not always express themselves in the way that God originally designed.
- Corruption, abuse, and greed are economic realities we see at play in the marketplace every day (we will explore this in the next chapter).
- Our misplaced trust in comfort, wealth, and security should be challenged as idolatry of any kind is a sin.

I'm suggesting that when we talk about "the economy," we must clearly understand what it is we are talking about, especially as Christians. The economy isn't impersonal. When we talk about devastating coronavirus statistics, we're talking about real *people*, not just lifeless numbers and graphs. When we talk about the economy, we're *also* talking about people—real, live, human people.

It should not be morally questionable to say you care about the economy. Those who pit caring for people against caring about the economy either don't understand economics or have an ulterior motive. In fact, by better understanding economics, I believe we can better love our neighbors.

ECONOMIC IDOLATRY

When critics push back on concern for "the economy," what they're really pushing back on is economic idolatry. As we explored previously, an idol isn't a gold statue. An idol is anything we find our identity in, anything we place our ultimate hope and trust in outside of God Himself. We humans are idol-making machines, and there is no doubt plenty of us have become worshippers of economic comfort and prosperity, especially in Western cultures and contexts.

But the things we idolize aren't normally evil in and of themselves. In fact, Tim Keller says idolatry is turning good things into ultimate things. I know women who idolize their children, yet it would be odd to argue that motherhood itself is problematic. The object of our idolatry is rarely the issue; it's the misuse or misplaced adoration of these things that becomes sinful.

When some hear conversations about "the economy," they envision Ebenezer Scrooge abusing his poor clerk with long hours and below-market wages, all the while extorting his neighbors with higher and higher interest rates and graceless demands for loan repayment.

Like Scrooge, many modern-day films and TV shows feature big business antagonists and powerful people leveraging the marketplace to take advantage of the little guy or wreak havoc on the environment. That triggers a rightful sense of injustice, so for many "the economy" instinctively become synonymous with the love of money and power, corporate greed, and the rich guy coveting a new vacation home in the Hamptons.

"Everything is marred by sin, but everything also has an original sacred design."

But we can't define the marketplace by its sinful expression any more than we can ascribe that same broken storyline to government, science, education, healthcare, or any other sphere of life. Everything is marred by sin, but everything also has an original sacred design.

ECONOMICS IS ABOUT PEOPLE

When people express concern for the health of the economy, they're not *inherently* talking about rich people and their retirement accounts. We *have* to see clearer than the caricature.

At its root, the economy is the sacred intertwining of human lives in mutual service to one another. It's about image-bearers leveraging their unique makeup and God-given giftings to meet a need in someone else's life. The economy is about mutual service, interdependence, people serving and adding value to one another. The economy is a beautiful means by which we can live out the Great Commandment—to worship God and love our neighbor.

Is the economy broken by sin? Absolutely. Everything is. But we can't allow the sinful expression of the marketplace to hijack its true, sacred design.

There's a reason business and entrepreneurship are now being used as missions strategy all over the world today (more on this in Part 3). Good business fosters relationships and human connection. It leaves people with more together than they could ever have had separately. And that is a beautiful conduit for the gospel.

The coronavirus pandemic of 2020 exposed our idolatry of economic comfort and prosperity. God often uses suffering to show us the futility of all the places we've rooted ourselves outside of Him. For that, we all need to repent and return to Jesus.

But the marketplace is not some inanimate, amoral object. Going to work every day is one of the foundational ways we honor God and love our neighbor. Don't buy into the broken caricature. The economy is the God-designed, people-serving, human-flourishing intertwining of lives in mutual service to one another. That's a sacred thing. It's right to care about the economy because when you care about the economy, you are caring about people and loving your neighbor.

– *Khana Underwear* –

The first time I learned about Khana I was sitting at a conference table with a group of students and professors at North Central University in Minneapolis. The dean of the business school, a long-time friend and legendary jokester, started the meeting by saying, "OK, let's talk about your underwear." After the students stopped laughing at my red-faced expression, I learned about a beautiful business created by a marketing student as part of her senior project.

Shayna Fowler fell in love with Uganda during college. While visiting the East African nation, she learned that many school-age girls miss up to one week of school per month because their underwear is inadequate for managing menstruation. Many of these girls end up dropping out of school completely after they start their period. She had to do something.

Shayna worked with some friends to develop "the world's most powerful pair of panties." Made specifically to help girls manage their menstruation, the underwear is distributed to school-age girls across Uganda along with washable pads and menstruation education materials. It's already making a difference.

Khana is a hybrid business-charity model. You can donate directly to the cause, or women can purchase Khana-brand underwear for themselves in the U.S. Faith-inspired entrepreneurs are solving real-world problems through the marketplace. Through manufacturing underwear, Shayna Fowler is honoring God and loving her neighbor. That is definitely one powerful pair of panties.

10

Greed Is Not a
Business Problem

Greed is not a financial issue. It's a heart issue.

ANDY STANLEY

H ave you noticed who the villains often are in many movies
and TV shows?

The Lego Movie was terrorized by Lord Business who longed to
destroy Lego World by gluing all the pieces together.

And Spongebob Squarepant's tyrannical boss, Mr. Krabs, the
owner of Bikini Bottom's favorite diner, talks to his money, sleeps
with his money, and will sell out his own family just to make an
extra buck.

The 1980s film *Wall Street* introduced us to the nefarious Gordon Gecko, the character who coined the infamous catchphrase "greed is good." To this day, it still defines what many believe is the driving force of the free market.

It's not a surprise when the antagonist turns out to be the evil corporate business guy who wants to destroy the neighborhood park where all the kids play after school so he can build a chemical plant that will kill all the trees and make people sick, just so he can build a bigger mansion and eventually take over the world. In popular culture, big business is consistently caricaturized as the tool of choice for money-hungry power brokers that want to take advantage of other people.

Part of this could be an anti-business agenda from our friends in Hollywood, but caricatures are usually stereotypical exaggerations of real-life tendencies. We connect with them because there is at least some level of truth behind it all.

Google the phrase "corporate greed" for some real-life examples like:

- Bernie Madoff was a stockbroker and former chairman of NASDAQ who orchestrated the largest Ponzi scheme in world history. Investors lost a jaw-dropping $65 billion dollars through their dealings with him, and he is now spending 150 years in jail for his crimes.
- Enron was an energy company that employed 29,000 people and was once considered a blue-chip stock. They hid massive financial losses and bankruptcies from their board of directors and pressured their accounting

firm to ignore their audit findings. Twenty-one people went to jail because of the Enron scandal, 90-year-old accounting powerhouse Arthur Anderson was forced out of business, and 85,000 employees across multiple industries lost their jobs.

- During the mortgage banking crisis of 2008, brokers were approving thousands of mortgages for people they knew could not afford them, all to ensure they hit their lavish bonus numbers. It was rumored that some of these shysters even filled out loan applications in the names of their pet cats so they could hit their quotas.

These are just a few of the devastating stories of greed parading around in business attire. When you imagine a greedy person, my guess is that one of these images of an evil corporate tycoon isn't far from your mind. The business world has an undeniable and verifiable history of greed, there is no doubt.

IS BUSINESS THE PROBLEM?

Does this mean business is inherently selfish? Does this mean business is just some sinful, kill-or-be-killed institution that man invented to exert power and survive in this fallen world? Is business really synonymous with greed? Does engaging in the marketplace actually *make* people greedy?

I'd like to offer a different take.

Greed is not a business problem; it's a worship problem.

That's so important I will say it again.

Greed is not a business problem; it's a worship problem.

Idolatry, the worship of anything other than God, is the root of all sin. Idolatry is the evil hijacker of God's intended design for His creation and the creator of deceptive counterfeits. The business world is not the enemy; idolatry is the enemy. Business is not greedy; idolatry is greedy.

The Apostle Paul laid it out plainly for the church in Ephesus:

> *You can be sure that no immoral, impure, or greedy person will inherit the Kingdom of Christ and of God.* **For a greedy person is an idolater, worshiping the things of this world.** *(Ephesians 5:5 NLT, emphasis mine)*

Paul obviously thought this was important because he repeated the exact same warning to the church in Colossae:

> *So put to death the sinful, earthly things lurking within you. Have nothing to do with sexual immorality, impurity, lust, and evil desires.* **Don't be greedy, for a greedy person is an idolater, worshiping the things of this world.** *(Colossians 3:5 NLT, emphasis mine)*

You see, greed is not a business problem. Greed is not a marketplace problem. Greed is not a capitalism problem. Greed is a worship problem!

When we worship the things of this world, we give them the ultimate place in our lives, a throne they were never intended to occupy. Instead of playing the subservient, God-honoring, people-serving, human-flourishing role they were designed for, the things of this world become the actual objects of our affection. Sin is not doing bad things; it is mis-using good things.

Money is a great tool, but an oppressive master. Happiness is a beautiful byproduct, but a dangerous pursuit. When power is used to willfully serve others, it manifests beauty. When power becomes our ultimate objective, it turns on us and becomes a weapon of destruction.

Greed manifests when money becomes the object of our trust.

Greed manifests when temporal happiness takes precedence over obedience.

Greed manifests when power becomes the source of our identity.

A greedy person is an idolater, worshipping the things of this world. (Ephesians 5:5 NLT)

THE MARKETPLACE IS ABOUT GIVING, NOT TAKING

There's a common and almost instinctive belief in much of modern Western culture that business is solely about making money, a mechanism uniquely designed for extracting value. Many define business success in terms of how much one person can take from others and horde for themselves. As we've seen in earlier examples, this kind of abuse undoubtedly exists, so it's little wonder that so many find business synonymous with greed.

This intertwining of business and greed even seems to make some Christians feel uncomfortable about what they do, as if their marketplace jobs are just an unfortunate reality they have to endure in this sinful world; this is their lot in this temporal life until Jesus returns and saves us from this greedy, evil, business-shackled economic reality. Thank God we will go to heaven someday so we can peacefully sit on clouds and play those harps!

It's time for marketplace Christians to stop being shaped by these counterfeits.

At its core, good business is first and foremost about what I can *give* to others. It doesn't start with what can I get, but how can I *add value* to other people and the world around me? It's about seeing a need and meeting it, recognizing a problem and solving it, identifying something that is missing from the world and creating it.

Rabbi Daniel Lapin, a popular Jewish voice in the realm of business and economics, loves to call dollar bills "certificates of appreciation." The more people I serve, the more value I add, the more problems I solve, the more certificates of appreciation I get in return. I love that imagery for business and the marketplace. Don't buy into the distortion created by the idolatry of money, power, and happiness. The gospel redeems all things, including the work of our hands.

HARVESTING ALL THE WAY TO THE EDGES

How do we combat this idolatry of greed? Anytime we become aware of idolatry of any kind in our lives, repentance is always the way back home. To repent means to "turn and go the other way." Repentance is core to the gospel and should be a daily practice for all believers.

In the words of the old hymn: "Prone to wander, Lord, I feel it, prone to leave the God I love."[15]

"We confront our greed with giving."

The "idol factories" of our hearts must be consistently confronted and brought under the endless grace of Jesus. But alongside this ongoing call to repentance, there are proactive ways to tear down these greedy imposters. It starts with allowing the gospel to resurrect a spirit of generosity in you.

We confront our greed with giving.

There's an Old Testament passage that is rarely referenced in the context of marketplace generosity, but it fits nicely here.

> *When you harvest the crops of your land, do not harvest the grain along the edges of your fields, and do not pick up what the harvesters drop. It is the same with your grape crop—do not strip every last bunch of grapes from the vines, and do not pick up the grapes that fall to*

---

15   "Come, Thou Fount of Every Blessing." Written by Robert Robinson in 1758.

the ground. Leave them for the poor and the foreigners living among you. I am the LORD your God. (Leviticus 19:9–10 NLT)

As God established the way His people should live in honor to Him and in love to one another, He commanded them not to harvest their fields all the way to the edges and not to strip their vines bare of all their fruit. He told them to willfully walk away from business assets that belonged to them so that those in need could also be blessed by their harvest. God created "multiple bottom lines" to define marketplace success, and one of them was generosity.

GIVING FROM OVERFLOW

I recently had dinner with a wildly successful Christian real estate developer. His companies have been responsible for the construction of billions in commercial and residential properties all over the country. As his success grew, he felt compelled not just to give away portions of his profits, but to freely share his models and strategies with younger developers who wanted to learn the business. He began giving away both the resources and skillset they needed to build wealth for themselves, and he taught them how to give forward from their newly created assets to build God's kingdom.

Over dinner he said to me, "I love what you guys do with your missions-focused nonprofit housing company. I would be willing to share my whole playbook with you so you can use it to build resources for the Kingdom." He's tearing down the idol of greed through radical, consistent, open-handed generosity.

GIVING FROM LACK

When my wife was in college, a missionary named David Grant came and spoke at Southeastern University where she was attending. As he shared about the great need for the gospel in Southeast Asia, the Holy Spirit spoke to Mandy and told her to give $1,000 to his ministry. There was one problem—she had no money. Every penny to her name was already committed to her portion of her tuition obligation. But she held a deep conviction that God was speaking to her and stepped out in faith.

A few weeks later, she was on a flight back to Indianapolis, and she struck up a conversation with the woman sitting next to her. As it turned out, her husband played for the NBA's Orlando Magic and this woman was in need of a regular babysitter for her kids. Mandy was nearly inseparable from this woman and her children over the next few years, not only earning more than enough money to fulfill her missions commitment, but also fostering a friendship that allowed her to share the light of the love of Jesus with the family as she cared for their kids.

Freely you have received; freely give. (Matthew 10:8 NIV)

We don't give to get. As we learn to live with open hands, to embrace multiple bottom lines, to avoid harvesting "all the way to the edges," we rebel against the idol of greed and turn our everyday work into the beautiful demonstration and proclamation of the gospel it was created to be. Whether we have little or much, radical generosity should be the default posture of every believer.

There's an approach to financial management often taught in Christian circles. Give ten percent, save ten percent, and live on the other eighty percent. I love this strategy and have even taught it to my kids. But beyond all the dollars and cents, God wants our hearts. In reality, it *all* belongs to Him and that is our best starting point.

I heard someone once say that money is "congealed life." How we spend our money outwardly shows who we really are on the inside. The inside and the outside coalesce to form a satisfying whole. It's a reflection of how we order the things that are most important to us. In that way, it reveals what we are actually worshipping.

As marketplace believers, let's take back the marketplace from these greedy cultural caricatures. Greed is not a business problem, it's a *worship* problem. How is God calling you back to right worship with your resources?

– Blankets as Mission –

My friend Amy and I grew up together on the west side of Indianapolis. Our families attended the same church and we garnered much of the same spiritual DNA throughout our upbringing, including a deep passion for the Great Commission.

Ultimately, Amy and her family moved to Southeast Asia to answer a personal call to full-time missions. It wasn't an easy move. Her husband found his place more easily in the male-dominated culture, while Amy struggled to connect with the local women and to feel at home in their new surroundings. Amy was a frustrated missionary that wanted to quit.

Until one day someone showed her an old sari (the traditional dress for women in the area) that had been "upcycled" into a beautiful blanket. As the daughter of an entrepreneur, that got Amy's faith-driven creativity percolating. She immediately had a vision of dozens of women sitting in circles on the floor, sewing together, talking about life, and encountering Jesus. "As we remake old saris into new blankets, what if Jesus begins remaking these women into who they were always created to be?"

Through a few divine encounters, Amy met a woman who taught her to sew the kantha, a special stitch used in this kind of blanket manufacturing. She also gained access to a supply of old sari material. After struggling for so long to relationally connect, Amy reached out to women in the local community with offers of employment. Today her BAM business empowers eighty women through above-market wages and a renewed sense of purpose.

These beautiful blankets are sold online and through local church relationships to support the women's salaries and the missionary work that is happening on the ground in this part of the world. Amy's business doesn't just produce blankets; it fosters relationships that are opening these women's hearts and pointing them to Jesus. Amy's vision of women connecting to one another and to the Lord has finally become a reality through the marketplace.

CHAPTER

11

Hiring and Firing to the Glory of God

And whatever you do or say, do it as a
representative of the Lord Jesus, giving
thanks through him to God the Father.

COLOSSIANS 3:17 (NLT)

I f economics is the intertwining of human lives in mutual
service to one another, then we will undoubtedly impact
the trajectory of other peoples' lives as we work together in the
marketplace. How we hire—and fire—people is a huge question
for believers looking to live out their faith at work. How do we
steward our power over someone's employment situation in light
of the Great Commandment in a way that glorifies God and loves
our neighbor as ourselves?

There are plenty of books that can help you with the practical details of hiring and firing. My intent here is simply to illuminate how the gospel resurrects our marketplace activities, so we're going to focus more on the redemptive impact of the gospel in the hiring and firing process. I will attempt to do that through two stories. One is warm and fuzzy, and the other is gut-wrenching. It's through the lens of these real-life experiences that I hope to bring our work and the Great Commandment into focus.

A GOOD HIRE

Konica is one of our company's best property managers. She oversees CRF's largest apartment community, a 424-unit, multi-phase campus on the near west side of Indianapolis. A vast majority of these apartments are what we call "deep subsidy." These are programs aimed at providing quality affordable housing for those with very low incomes.

Konica has proven to be tougher than nails when dealing with difficult situations in the community. She's fearless, yet underneath her bold exterior, her faith in Jesus keeps her soft and sensitive to the needs of others. I've seen it over and over again in how she approaches her job each day. One key hiring decision she made a few years back puts her empathy and spiritual sensitivity on full display. It's also one of my favorite stories to come out of our company's three-decade history.

Marlena had lived at Cloverleaf Apartments for almost ten years. She was on Section 8, a government subsidized housing program that helps low-income residents pay their rent. Section 8 requires extensive paperwork, background checks, and income verifications, and these forms have to be completed and updated constantly. It can be an overwhelming process for the resident and for our compliance staff.

Each time Marlena came into the office, Konica's team noticed how up to speed she was on all her paperwork. One time, she even caught an error the staff had made and helped to correct it. She knew all the forms thoroughly and seemed to understand the program as well as the management team.

Marlena was a great resident. She wanted a more stable life and a better income; she just needed an opportunity. When Konica's compliance director was promoted to the home office, she approached Marlena to see if she was interested in the job.

"I'm on Section 8," she replied. "Why would you want me for a job like that?"

But Konica saw the *imago Dei* in Marlena. "I see more in you," she said. "You've just never had an opportunity. Come work with us."

Marlena started working as a compliance officer for $11 per hour. In the same rental office where she once filled out her own Section 8 paperwork, she now sat on the other side of the desk helping countless other residents work through their complex forms and document requirements. Slowly but surely, Marlena became one of the best on-site compliance minds in our company. So good, in fact, that a new opportunity came calling.

Marlena received an incredible job offer from a company called Quadel that helps apartment communities like ours interface with the Department of Housing and Urban Development. Today, she makes three times what she made working for us, and our entire company is celebrating with her.

Konica honored God and loved her neighbor when she hired Marlena. It was a beautiful expression of Great Commandment. As Konica likes to say, "I want to use my leadership position to reach back and pull others forward." She didn't see the same status the world had stamped on Marlena. She saw the image of God.

A DIFFICULT SEPARATION

Not all employment stories are as heartwarming as Marlena's. Thankfully, I haven't had to terminate too many people during my leadership tenure, but the few separations I've had to initiate were terribly painful. The toughest by far was a senior leadership position. This was someone I trusted to oversee others on our staff and to do it in a way that reflected our culture and our faith.

I was initially attracted to this hire because of his experience and skillset. It was completely different than mine. I felt his direct and somewhat confrontational demeanor would be a great supplement to my more encouragement-based leadership style.

For about a year, I felt great about what was happening. We were identifying problems better, running our operations through a rubric of new key performance indicators, and holding each other accountable for outcomes. But slowly, I began to hear stories of relational strain and power plays that made me uncomfortable. I liked what was happening, but I hated the way it was unfolding.

Initially, I pushed it aside. "People just don't like being held accountable," I told myself. "You've been so 'nice' over the years. People have taken advantage of you and the company. This is just what happens when you bring strong, outcome-based leadership into the mix."

I was wrong.

By God's grace, a series of unfortunate events shined a light on some things our team was afraid to tell me and made it very clear what

"How does my faith inform the termination of a key employee?"

I needed to do. The facts were indisputable, but I still agonized over the decision for an entire weekend. This guy was wrong, and he was hurting us, but I desperately wanted to show God's grace in the moment. How could I love this man and fire him at the same time? How does my faith inform the termination of a key employee? My stomach was in knots.

That's when the Holy Spirit led me to 1 Corinthians 13. The "love chapter" of the Bible is usually reserved for weddings and marriage retreats, but the Lord illuminated a key phrase often buried by the feel-good verses. It lit up the page like it was written in neon lights.

Love is patient and kind; love does not envy or boast; it is not arrogant or rude. It does not insist on its own way; it is not irritable or resentful; **it does not rejoice at wrongdoing, but rejoices with the truth.** *Love bears all things, believes all things, hopes all things, endures all things.* (1 Corinthians 13:4–7, emphasis mine)

Love "does not rejoice at wrongdoing."

We confuse love with sentimentality. Loving our neighbor doesn't automatically translate into doing what they would prefer us to do. True love isn't always underscored by a schmaltzy soaring string section. That kind of love is reserved for the Hallmark movie channel. Sometimes the "love your neighbor soundtrack" is written in a minor key.

Love—true love—seeks the other's good. That kind of love is really messy at times. It's down and dirty, in the weeds, and far from warm and fuzzy. In that moment, the good of this particular employee (and the good of our team as a whole) was to not allow him to work for us anymore.

It was one of the hardest conversations I've ever had to have with another human being, but ultimately, I knew I was loving my neighbor by *not* rejoicing in his wrongdoing. I was caring for him and the rest of our staff by holding him accountable for his actions and severing our working relationship. I truly believe that we loved him by firing him.

We affirmed the good he did for our company, encouraged the *imago Dei* that was still stamped on his life, and tried to make his transition as easy as possible. I wish I could tell you that the relationship is still intact, but we hold no animosity and continue to wish him the best. I'm certain that we stumbled along the way, but I truly think we did our best to glorify God through the termination of a staff member.

A STRANGE DINNER GUEST

I was at lunch with another Christian apartment owner recently. As we talked about the differences between our nonprofit and for-profit setups, he told me a story I will never forget. At our meal that day, he was eating a light lunch because he and his team were making dinner for a former employee and taking it to his house after work. Due to a recent surgery, friends and family had started a meal train, and his former co-workers wanted to show their support for their former teammate. What made the overture unique was that this guy had been fired by the company just a few months earlier.

"Isn't that going to be a little awkward?" I asked him.

"Yeah, maybe," he replied, "but we're committed to do everything we can to preserve the human relationship even when the employment relationship has to end."

That stuck with me.

As followers of Jesus, we believe in the sacredness of the marketplace. But "thorns and thistles" still mar God's original design. Living out the Great Commandment in the workplace certainly isn't neat and tidy, but when we strive to see the *imago Dei* in those around us and commit to the true biblical definition of love, we can bring a little taste of God's kingdom into our office culture. We can hire and even fire to the glory of God.

– *CrossFit Community* –

Health and fitness are an obsession in many cultures. People want to be in shape. This rising global demand is a market opportunity that BAM missionaries are seizing. The CrossFit brand is already a global phenomenon. Along with burpees, box jumps, and overhead kettle ball swings, CrossFit also meets one of mankind's most fundamental longings: community.

CrossFit programs are tight-knit communities. The friendships and deep desire for belonging drive the obsessive accountability to the workout regiments. Participants challenge each other, cheer for each other, and often end up hanging out together outside the gym as well. It's a made-to-order BAM business model, and it's being leveraged for the Kingdom in multiple countries around the world.

In North Africa, a young Muslim student recently followed his CrossFit missionary-instructor to his car after class. It was Ramadan, and many of the students like to work out right before heading home to break the day's fast with their families. The two were making small talk when the student unexpectedly began to ask deep questions about Jesus. Those questions expanded into additional questions about the church, life after death, and countless other spiritual things. The conversation lasted for two hours, and now these two men meet regularly to study the *Injil* (Arabic for the New Testament).

God is using CrossFit gyms to demonstrate and proclaim the gospel and to plant the church among unreached people groups around the world.

CHAPTER

12

The Rhythms of Work and Rest

There is a virtue in work, and there is a virtue in rest. Use both and overlook neither.

ALAN COHEN

At first glance, the subject of work-rest rhythm doesn't seem to fit into the Great Commandment framework. But learning to rest well is actually part of honoring God with our work, and so I think it's worth some discussion here.

On one of my first trips to the Middle East, I found myself sitting in a room full of missionaries. These beautiful men and women, part of a pioneer missions movement called Live Dead, live, work, and run small businesses in some of the most unreached and anti-Christian cultures on the globe. They were gathered from around the region as part of their monthly training, to worship together, to encourage one another, and to hear from leadership about staying focused on the task at hand.

I'll never forget that night, lifting my voice and my hands in worship to Jesus on the top floor of a North African office building not far from where the Arab Spring skirmishes had erupted just a few years earlier. My friend Dick led the gathering and capped the night with a long list of challenges for the missionary teams.

One of his key points has stuck with me to this day: "Some of you don't know how to *rest*," he said, "and you need to repent of that sin, ask Jesus to forgive you, and embrace a healthier rhythm in your life."

Then he turned the tables in a way I wasn't expecting: "But some of you don't know how to *work*. You need to repent of that sin, ask Jesus to forgive you, and get much more active in the work you're here to do."

In our manic, Western, capitalistic culture, many of us know the guilt of not resting well. But Dick reminded me that not working well is a sin, too. It's work and rest, rest and work. We honor God by learning how to do both of these things well and in a way that reflects our complete faith and trust in the redemptive power of the gospel.

THE DISCIPLINE OF REST

I looked at my calendar recently and noticed something unusual: There was nothing there. There were zero colored appointment blocks in the Saturday column. It was glorious discovery that I decided to embrace fully.

I slept until I naturally woke up (which, unfortunately, isn't very late for me anymore). I spent the morning drinking coffee and reading some good books. I put my feet up for a little college football in the afternoon. I had a nice dinner out with the family that evening. It was a beautiful, restful, re-energizing sabbath.

For me, that kind of rest is a discipline. I migrate toward busyness. I feel good when I'm accomplishing things. I'm driven by checking the next thing off that never ending to-do list. But rest isn't just a nice idea. We're actually *commanded* to do it. Taking a day away from work each week began in Genesis 2 when the Creator of the universe modeled it for us Himself.

*On the seventh day God had finished his work of creation, so he **rested** from all his work. And God blessed the seventh day and declared it holy, because it was the day when he **rested** from all his work of creation. (Genesis 2:2–3 NLT, emphasis mine)*

Not only is rest a gift from God; it's also a regular reminder that the world doesn't rise and fall our ability to get things done. We are needy people who require rest and find our strength in our dependence on Jesus. Every time I get a little too self-reliant, the

Lord reminds me that my humanity requires me to shut down and sleep for twenty-five to thirty percent of my life. That's humility at its finest.

THE FLIP SIDE

While this gift of rest is something our American culture inherently struggles with (a tendency that has only been enhanced by technology's ability to keep us virtually connected to our work at all times), there seems to be an emerging counterculture movement that almost celebrates rest as the ultimate pursuit of human existence. This is perplexing to me, as Scripture makes our calling to work and keep God's creation ever so clear.

> *The Lord God took the man and put him in the Garden of Eden to work it and take care of it. (Genesis 2:15 NIV)*

As is often the case with our broken human tendencies, our urge to self-correct a legitimate abuse swings the pendulum to a whole different kind of abuse. While work is broken by sin, while manic productivity has obviously become an idol in many cultures, while we can wrongly place our hope and our identity in our career, work itself is not the enemy of our souls. In fact, we were created to work! Not to earn our name and God's favor (that work was finished by Jesus), but to honor God and serve our neighbors with the work of our hands.

You and I are capable of making an idol out of anything in this life. Even the good things. Perhaps especially the good things! But while we've all seen countless examples of the workaholic dad that chronically misses his kid's basketball games, or the stressed-out entrepreneur that loses her family in pursuit of her start-up dream, the truth is that we can make an idol out of our leisure time and even our families, too.

In Mark 2:27, Jesus reminds us that "the Sabbath was made for man, not man for the Sabbath." We were not made for rest; rest is a gift to us from God. We were made to dream, create, cultivate, to make culture and add value to the world around us in big and small ways. We were created to "work and take care of" God's creation as His vice-regents and image-bearers. That mandate is meant to be lived out in the boardroom and the family room.

> **"Work and rest are not enemies— they're partners."**

Work and rest are not enemies—they're partners. Work is part of our creation mandate. While our work is a vital part of God's Great Story, rest is our consistent daily and weekly reminder that we are most certainly not the authors.

Here's my encouragement to all of us today: Be aware of your sinful ability to turn work into a self-salvation project, but don't make work into your enemy. Learn to dance to the rhythm.

Some of you don't know how to rest, and you need to repent of that sin and ask Jesus to forgive you. But some of you don't know how to work, and you need to repent of *that* sin and ask Jesus to forgive you.

WHO ARE YOU?

Have you succumbed to our Western culture's margin-less worship of work? Is work where you find your identity and seek to make a name for yourself? Do you struggle to turn off your work and focus on your family, friends, and mental health? Then repent and embrace rest as the gift that it is. The world can get along just fine without you for a few hours each week. That's good to remember.

Or have you made work into the enemy? If so, then stop it. You were created to work. Whether you're closing a multimillion-dollar deal, performing brain surgery, folding laundry, assembling a piece of IKEA furniture, mowing the grass, or even changing a diaper, serving others and adding value to the world around you (in both exceptional and simple ways) are part of the human vocation. Rest is a gift, but you were made to work! This is key to how we fulfill the Great Commandment to honor God and love our neighbor. We do it through the work of our hands.

– *The Global Gig Economy* –

I have a friend who spent years writing, editing, and publishing for well-known magazines and publications here in the United States. Most of her employers would be recognizable to many of you. But her heart for global missions opened new doors for her writing and missional calling to collide.

She now lives in the Middle East, where her writing and editing business continues to flourish in a cross-cultural context. She continues to do great work for clients around the world, but this new strategic location also gives her access to people who need Jesus. Today, she is connected with a hub of BAM missionaries who leverage their marketplace skills to get much-needed work visas. Those visas allow them to plant themselves among strategic unreached people groups around the world.

These types of gig-entrepreneurs are a huge asset to Great Commission efforts across the globe. Perhaps you are a writer or editor, a graphic designer, videographer, web developer, or make a living through other kinds of "portable" gig-work.

There are huge opportunities to move your base of operations to strategic unreached areas of the world. There you can partner with teams of other BAM missionaries taking the gospel to those with no access to Jesus. The need is great, the opportunities are endless, and your portable gig-work just might make you a prime candidate for this kind of calling.

13

Retirement Is Not in the Bible

*America is the first culture in jeopardy of
amusing itself to death.*

JOHN PIPER

CRF Affordable Housing has been in the apartment management business for thirty years. Like any management company, we have our share of difficult tenants. Anytime hundreds of people live in close proximity to one another, conflict is bound to happen. I often tease our on-site staff that they should pitch a reality TV show to the Discovery Channel.

CRF provides affordable housing to somewhere between five and six thousand people at any given moment across our apartment portfolio. With that many residents living in such close proximity to one another, where would you predict the most conflict to arise?

At our senior apartment communities, hands down.

I recently heard about an "assault with a deadly cookie" that took place following a highly contested bingo match. House rules say that any one player can only win three games during the course of play. When one man cried "bingo!" for the fourth time, a group of ladies sitting at the next table adamantly reminded him of the non-negotiable win limit. A heated argument ensued that ultimately culminated with an oatmeal-raisin to the face! (In fairness, no one likes to eat oatmeal-raisin cookies anyway.)

MODERN RETIREMENT

I believe a number of these out-of-proportion meltdowns in our senior communities have at least something to do with our modern Western understanding of retirement. Because so many of us, even in the Christian community, have completely misunderstood God's original design and purpose for our everyday work, we spend our entire lives trying to get rid of it.

Endure forty-plus years of work misery, maybe put some money into an IRA or 401(k) along the way, pay into social security, and when you reach the magic age of 65, then you finally enter that stage of life when you no longer have to serve anyone but yourself. If you're lucky, maybe you can afford to do it in a warmer climate, too.

It's not that ceasing traditional, full-time work is problematic. It's the "crossing some oppressive subservient finish line so we can live out our final days effectively thinking only about ourselves" paradigm that must be examined and challenged. That vision of retirement is actually a forsaking of the Great Commandment. Not to mention, humans get weird when they only think about themselves—they start throwing cookies at each other at bingo games.

BIBLICAL RETIREMENT

My friend Chuck recently retired from his long career in the corporate world. Soon after, he penned some of his initial reflections that we shared on The Stone Table website. I love how Chuck frames it: "The Bible never speaks of 'retirement.' There's no mention of any biblical character quitting his fishing or farming job and heading off to 'Dead Sea Beach' or sailing off to some distant island with no God-inspired purpose in mind."[16]

It's true. The only reference we have of anyone in the Bible "retiring" is about the Levites:

> And the LORD spoke to Moses, saying, "This applies to the Levites: from twenty-five years old and upward they shall come to do duty in the service of the tent of meeting. And from the age of fifty years they shall withdraw from the duty of the service and serve no more. They minister to their brothers in the tent of meeting by keeping guard, but they shall do no service." (Numbers 8:23–26)

While the Levites stopped their official service within the daily activities of the temple, they continued to minister to the

---

16   Chuck Rapp. "Retirement Is Not in the Bible." The Stone Table. http://www.the-stonetable.org/retirement-is-not-in-the-bible/ (accessed April 20, 2021).

community by "keeping guard" for the rest of their lives. Another translation says they could "continue to assist" their brothers in the work.

If work is one of the primary ways we are called to fulfill the Great Commandment, then, while the work itself may change, the call to honor God and love our neighbor has no expiration date. I've had the joy of watching this healthy tension unfold in the lives of people I love and respect.

CORPORATE RETIREMENT

I just mentioned my friend Chuck. He worked for over four decades in the corporate world as a project and IT manager. Chuck is two decades ahead of me, and from an outsider's perspective, he was the prototypical high-capacity corporate leader. Other than a short, midlife season of full-time ministry work in Brussels, Belgium, Chuck and his family were faithful to their jobs, devoted to their church, committed mentors to many, and passionate supporters of global missions.

"The call to honor God and love our neighbor has no expiration date."

When their financial advisor painted a stable post-career financial picture, Chuck and his wife Pam decided it was time to move into a new season of life. While Chuck embraced his job as a gift from God and a way to honor Him and serve others, he had long ago realized it was not the source of his identity. "Work is just getting in the way of all the things I feel called to do," he told his boss.

He took the leap, not into the modern understanding of retirement, but into a different way of serving the Kingdom. Chuck began volunteering his time with One Mission Society. A few initial responsibilities have now turned into serving and overseeing multiple missionaries and ministries on the continent of Africa. So much for slowing down! Chuck realizes his experience and abilities still have value to add to the Kingdom, so what he used to engage with his spare time has now moved front and center. Retirement wasn't quitting; rather, it was stepping into a new way of fulfilling the Great Commandment.

MINISTRY RETIREMENT

As I mentioned near the beginning of the book, I grew up under a global missions pastor. Tom Paino was a powerful presence in our lives, and we looked up to him in every way. I remember the day he announced his retirement from full-time pastoral ministry. We didn't know who could ever fill his oversized shoes.

But while Pastor Tom certainly enjoys golf and warm weather, he had zero intention of riding off into traditional retirement sunset. In fact, he had been planning his life after pastoring for some time. He started a missions fundraising nonprofit called Action2000 that would become his main focus after the daily responsibilities of leading a large church were finally over.

The focus of Action2000 was to recruit his business and other high net worth relationships to fund priority missions projects in strategic areas around the world. It was Tom's work through Action2000 (which changed its name to ActioNow after the turn of the millennium) that inspired the genesis of CRF Affordable Housing. ActioNow was the main recipient of CRF's charitable missions dollars for over twenty years.

While Pastor Tom left the daily grind of full-time pastoring, he remained passionately (some might even say obsessively) engaged in ministry work, traveling, fundraising, and speaking around the world.

When he approached me in 2014 about "slowing down a little bit," he was 91 and had just returned from overseas trips to Spain and Cuba. He officially passed the baton with the launch of The Stone Table in 2015. To this day I tease him that he's likely to outlive me so I'm not sure why he ever stopped. He officially retired from our board of directors at age 95, but it's still not unusual for him to call the office to see if we have any extra funds laying around because he's been working with a missionary on a side project. At a holiday gathering last year, he shared the outline of a sermon he had been working on and a word he felt the Lord had given him for the church. I fully expect a chariot of fire to sweep down from heaven and carry him away. If I've learned one thing from my childhood pastor, it's run to the finish line and keep adding whatever value you can until your very last breath.

ENTREPRENEURIAL RETIREMENT

I returned to CRF in 2012 to slowly begin taking the reins of day-to-day leadership from my dad. He was in his late-60s at the time, and a clear succession plan wasn't really in place. He and the board knew it was time to think about the next season of CRF's success.

We planned for a long cross-fade, but even as I begin to shoulder more of the leadership responsibility, my dad realized something: He enjoys work. "What am I going to do all day if I don't come here?" he continues to ask me. Even as his role shifted to more strategy and oversight, he knows he still has value to add and wants to keep adding it. He is sitting in his office across the way from mine working on financial projections as I write. No one here will argue with that. He has made the shift well.

Not everyone has the luxury my dad does to remain with an organization he helped to pioneer and build. Sometimes you're forced to walk away because you can't do the work anymore or because the vision and direction of the company has shifted out from underneath you. But what I've seen so clearly from my father is a desire to keep adding value, to keep pushing forward, to keep pouring out. While he may not serve in the same way he used to, he's most certainly continuing to "stand guard."

BIBLICAL RETIREMENT

While all of us will eventually retire from the day jobs we hold today, no follower of Jesus ever gets their gold watch retirement party from the Great Commandment. The modern Western vision of a self-absorbed closing chapter to this life is found nowhere in Scripture. We honor God and serve and love our neighbor until our dying breath.

Does that mean it's wrong to slow down, change pace, play more golf, travel, spend more time with the grandkids, or buy a condo in Florida? Of course not! But I will challenge every believer to consider how they will run to the finish line. We were made to work, keep, and add value to the world around us. That commandment has no expiration date.

– *No Retirement Thompson* –

My friend John Thompson has a gift for business. When he and his wife Bonnie got married, John worked a minimum wage job as a janitor in the local Lafayette, Indiana school system. John and Bonnie loved the Lord and were faithful to Him with whatever they had, big or small. Like me, John grew up in a global missions church, so giving whatever he could to missions was always a high priority.

John and his brother then became award-winning car salesmen and launched out on their own founding Thompson Brothers Auto Sales. (Yes, even "used car salesman" is a vocation that can be redeemed by the gospel.)

As John got older, he began to dabble in the local real estate market. He had a knack for recognizing a deal and the guts to pull the trigger when others got cold feet. Over the last twenty years, John has bought and sold countless commercial and residential buildings, and now flips houses with his son. All the while, he's been consistently faithful to give to the work of the Kingdom and to the mission of God around the world. When a missions project emerges, John is usually the first one to pull out his checkbook.

Now well into his 60s, John and Bonnie could easily retire to Florida and play golf every day. But John said something to me recently that caught my attention. "Every time I think, 'Man, I'm tired. I should stop working so much,' I look at the next opportunity and think, 'Well, there's another $15,000 for missions. Let's do it.'"

John is one of my missions heroes. He would never think of himself that way, which is why I probably like him so much. He's been consistent, faithful, and generous his entire life. From the time he and Bonnie had nothing to the overflow of today, they see themselves as the supporting cast in God's Great Story. Their focus on honoring God and building His kingdom has never wavered. May the same be said of all of us, no matter the size of our bank accounts.

PART

III

Work and the Great Commission

*Go therefore and make disciples of all
nations, baptizing them in the name of the
Father and of the Son and of the Holy Spirit,
teaching them to observe all that I have
commanded you. And behold, I am with you
always, to the end of the age.*

MATTHEW 28:19–20

CHAPTER

14

What Is the Great Commission?

*Preach the gospel at all times, and since it's
necessary, use words.*

ED STETZER

B efore we dive deep into the impact of the marketplace on the global mission of God in the world, I want to unpack some of our core missions convictions. Smart people might call this our *missiology*, but I have a friend who still insists that's a made-up word. We'll call it Missions 101. Roll with me here while we look at some global missions foundations.

My childhood church "slow-baked" us in the Great Commission. We marinated in it like mom's Sunday pot roast in the oven. It was unavoidable. Flags of the nations all over the building, missionary pictures all over the walls, annual missions conventions with parades, ethnic cuisine, and international costumes, a massive globe sitting atop a coin fountain in the lobby. One of my closest high school friends spent his primary school years as a missionary in Bangladesh.

None of this was strange to us; it was just how we did church. Under the leadership of our globally driven pastor, not one Sunday sermon seemed to pass without an appeal to take the gospel to all the people of the world. The Bible describes a church of all nations, tribes, and tongues, and we were going to make sure we did our part to see that reality come to pass.

All these years later, that passion and drive hasn't changed one bit. That Great Commission calling isn't just for certain denominations or specialized "CIA operative" type Christians. Jesus' words were aimed at all of us. Take the last words of Jesus to His awestruck disciples as He ascended into heaven:

Then the eleven disciples left for Galilee, going to the mountain where Jesus had told them to go. When they saw him, they worshiped him—but some of them doubted! Jesus came and told his disciples, "I have been given all authority in heaven and on earth. Therefore, go and make disciples of all the nations, baptizing them in the name of the Father and the Son and the Holy Spirit. Teach these new disciples to obey all the commands I have given you. And be sure of this: I am with you always, even to the end of the age." (Matthew 28:16–20 NLT)

This is the Great Commission. This challenge is a sacred mandate from our Savior Himself. It was Jesus' final instructions to His followers, our forefathers in the faith, as He ascended into heaven.

Go.

Make disciples.

All nations.

AN INVITATION TO TEA

I traveled to Tanzania with my brother-in-law and a dear friend from Indiana who shares our passion for global missions. A missionary to the area and a local man named Gil had big plans for us. It started with a four-hour drive on dried-out riverbeds toward Lake Eyasi, a shallow salt lake in the Rift Valley just south of Serengeti National Park. We were on our way to visit the Datooga—Gil's people—a nomadic tribe that live in the Rift Valley region of central Tanzania.

Our Land Cruisers crested a hill that overlooked the Rift Valley. Off to the right side, we noticed a woman walking along the side of the makeshift road. As we drew closer, we could see that she was carrying an infant on her back in a cloth wrap. The baby didn't appear to be much more than a few months old. Gil decided to stop and talk with her. We took a break to stretch our legs as Gil and our missionary friend engaged her in conversation. Gil spoke with her in the local dialect while the missionary translated for us—and what I heard changed me forever.

The baby's nose and mouth were covered with crusted mucus. He had obviously been sick for a while, so this concerned mother was walking miles to visit the closest witchdoctor. This mix of folk medicine and dark spiritualism were all the healthcare most of these local tribespeople knew. Gil ministered to her and asked if we could pray for her and her baby. Through the translator, I heard him say, "We would like to introduce you to Jesus." Immediately, her eyes brightened. "I would *love* to meet him!" she exclaimed. "I will be back in my village later today. Can you bring him by? I will make some tea."

Our chuckles quickly turned to the sober assessment of the reality we had just encountered. I had read about people like this, about places like this. This woman and her people are referred to as an "unreached people group." But suddenly this wasn't some exotic story I was reading in a book or a magazine. Right there, in that moment, I was staring into the real-life eyes of a person I had only previously known as a statistic shared in missions conferences. This woman had literally never heard the name Jesus.

MAKE DISCIPLES AMONG WHO?

The word Jesus uses in the Great Commission, in His final charge to His disciples before ascending to heaven, is the Greek word *ethnos*. Most Western translators render *ethnos* as "nations," which is an understandable simplification. Digging deeper into the original language, we learn that *ethnos* refers to a grouping of people joined together by similar customs or culture. Missiologists call these groupings "people groups."

An individual nation (country) may be comprised of hundreds or even thousands of different people groups. And Jesus wants them all.

Missiologists estimate there are between 6,000 and 7,000 people groups in the world that are unreached with the gospel. In this case, "unreached" is defined as a population that is less than two percent Christian. It means there are not enough believers within the people group to catalyze their own movement to Jesus. In some cases, we can count the number of Jesus followers in these unreached people groups (or UPGs, for short) on one hand, and about 1,500 of these UPGs have absolutely no access to the gospel whatsoever. These aren't just areas with a small number of Christians; these are areas with no known Christians at all, no churches, no Bibles, no radio, etc.

No access.

A huge portion of the earth's population can be born, live their entire lives, and die without ever hearing the name of Jesus.

Estimates of this reality top three billion people.

Three billion unreached.

3,000,000,000.

Forty-two percent of the earth's population.

This is the greatest injustice in our world today. Yet according to the Joshua Project, only three percent of foreign missionaries and less than one percent of all missions giving goes to these unreached areas of the world.[17]

As the Western world becomes less Christian, we cannot allow the current cultural moods to neutralize our passion for global evangelism. We must demonstrate and proclaim the kingdom of God to those within arm's reach as well as to those who have never heard about Jesus and to those who have no chance of hearing unless we go to them. We must embrace Jesus' Great Commission to take the gospel in all its fullness to every *ethnos*. Regardless of what you do for a living, if you are a follower of Jesus, this is your vocation, too.

PREACH THE GOSPEL

Jesus longs for all the sin-separated people of the world, from every reached and unreached people group of the world, and with His Spirit alive in us, our heart must break for them, too. If our daily work is a partnership with God to bring His kingdom to earth, then in much the same way, the Great Commission is also a divine Kingdom partnership. God has trusted this mandate to us. Global missions is the mandate of every Christ follower. This is not just a call to "professional" pastors and missionaries. It's a command for all believers, including those who find themselves employed in the marketplace.

---

17   Only 0.1 percent of all Christian giving is directed toward mission efforts in the 38 most unevangelized countries in the world. Source: David B. Barrett and Todd M. Johnson. *World Christian Trends AD 30 – AD 2200: Interpreting the annual Christian Megacensus.* Associate ed. Christopher R. Guidry and Peter F. Crossing. Pasadena, CA: William Carey Library, 2001. Statistic found at www.aboutmissions.org/statistics.html.

That's why I was shocked when a recent Barna research study revealed that fifty-one percent of Christians could not identify the Great Commission.[18] In fairness, that phrase was never specifically used in Scripture, but the study clearly revealed the core concept was foreign to most professing Christians as well.

> **"Gospel proclamation has become toxic—even in the church."**

Even more disturbing, a similar survey also discovered that half of all millennial Christians believe that it's morally questionable to share your faith with another person who doesn't already share your belief.[19] Younger Christians aren't just apathetic toward evangelism—many actually think it's wrong. Faith is okay as long as it remains personal and private. On the sliding scale of the universally disdained, sharing your faith with others places you somewhere between unsolicited door-to-door salesmen and conspiracy theory email forwarder.

Gospel proclamation has become toxic—even in the church. What happened?

There's a quote attributed to St. Francis of Assisi that floats around the internet. It sounds noble to our modern ears: "Preach the gospel at all times, and if necessary, use words." The problem with this quote

---

18   *Translating the Great Commission: What Spreading the Gospel Means to U.S. Christians in the 21ˢᵗ Century.* Barna Group, 2018.

19   *Reviving Evangelism: Current Realities That Demand a New Vision for Sharing Faith.* Barna Group, 2019.

is that there is no record anywhere that St. Francis of Assisi actually said it. In actuality, Francis was a member of a *preaching* order of Catholic friars in Italy. He preached as many as five times each day. We can only assume he incorporated lots of words into his homily.

I prefer Ed Stetzer's rewrite of this faux Assisi quote: "Preach the gospel, and since it's necessary, use words."[20] We are called to make disciples of all nations. Making disciples requires verbal interaction, and verbal interaction requires words.

I understand some of the cynicism. It's tempting to define missions success by global salvation counts while ignoring the fullness of the gospel's transforming message. A new generation of Christians wants to correct what they see as an imperial celebration of converts while the social and economic impact of God's kingdom goes ignored in these same parts of the world, and even our own communities. The gospel really does redeem *all* things. We want sincere displays of that redeemed life underneath all the talking and rhetoric. We want to see transformation rather than just hear someone rant about it all the time.

But the results of these Barna Group studies appear to show a case of overcorrection. Instead of championing the fullness of Jesus' redemptive work, we've attempted to re-balance by removing the essential part of missions work. Yes, we must embody the whole gospel, but this doesn't mean we just "do good things" around the world. We must also speak about Jesus to

---

20   Ed Stetzer. "Preach the Gospel, and Since It's Necessary, Use Words." Christiani-tyToday.com. https://www.christianitytoday.com/edstetzer/2012/june/preach-gospel-and-since-its-necessary-use-words.html (accessed April 21, 2021).

every nation, tribe, and tongue. The good news is meant to be proclaimed—with our mouths.

DEMONSTRATION AND PROCLAMATION

Jesus Himself modeled this two-pronged approach: show it and preach it.

> *And he went throughout all Galilee, teaching in their synagogues and proclaiming the gospel of the kingdom and healing every disease and every affliction among the people. (Matthew 4:23)*

> *And Jesus went throughout all the cities and villages, teaching in their synagogues and proclaiming the gospel of the kingdom and healing every disease and every affliction. (Matthew 9:35)*

Jesus brought the wholeness and healing of the Kingdom with Him everywhere He went. He set right what was wrong in physical bodies, in relationships, and in whole communities.

As His vice-regents, that's not unlike what we do with the work of our hands. The transformational power of the gospel brings our sin-dead selves back to life, and that new life will manifest itself in tangible, visible ways. The gospel redeems the marketplace and turns it into a daily opportunity to fulfil the Great Commandment. As we love God and love our neighbor, we demonstrate that resurrection power of the gospel.

And that's the part of the gospel storyline that universally resonates, both inside and outside the faith. No one argues with higher quality healthcare, better education for kids, higher paying jobs, or the economic healing of our communities.

But Jesus didn't stop there. Yes, He demonstrated the Kingdom, but He also proclaimed it.

So must we.

WHEN JESUS MESSES UP YOUR MISSIONS WORK

But that's really the problem, isn't it? Jesus. He tends to mess up the modern, acceptable view of missions. Let's face it. It's much easier to leave Jesus out of missions work altogether. He just gums up the works, makes things awkward, and creates controversy.

As part of an organization that mobilizes business for missions work around the world, I feel this in real ways every day. I'm proud of all of our work, but I've noticed something interesting. When I share with our staff (many who are not Christians) about the missions work we do, it's easy to talk to them about freeing women from sexual slavery, investing in schools and medical clinics, and helping to start micro-businesses around the world. It's the stories about church planting and the proclamation of Jesus as the way, truth, and life that are harder to craft. The excitement quickly dissipates into uncomfortable silence. "Why did you have to go and bring *Him* up?"

That leaves me in an interesting spot and pondering what will likely be a controversial statement for some of you: *Missions must ultimately lead to the proclamation of Jesus Christ and the establishment of the church, or it isn't really missions.*

I know, I know. Some of you are rushing to your Bible (or the latest trendy Christian magazine article) to show me why I'm wrong. But not only is the gospel to be proclaimed, it cannot be proclaimed without pointing to Jesus. There is no good news of the Kingdom without the life, death, resurrection, and ascension of the Savior. It's the Great Story, rooted in history, that must be told. The late missiologist Lesslie Newbigin said it this way: "When the message of the kingdom is divorced from the person of Jesus, it becomes a program or an ideology, but not a gospel."[21]

We humans have a unique ability to overcorrect, and today's generation is understandably energized by "doing good." That is a beautiful thing. We are not saved *by* good works, but we are most certainly saved *for* them. We must "do good," serve the poor, respond to the oppressed, care for the orphan, widow, and least of these, and pursue biblical justice. I can quote you all those scriptures, too.

We are most certainly called to honor God and love our neighbor, to demonstrate the resurrection power of the gospel to a broken world. But if the proclamation of the gospel and the declaration of

---

21   Lesslie Newbigin. *The Gospel in a Pluralistic Society.* Grand Rapids, MI: Wm. B. Eerdmans Publishing, 1989. 108.

Jesus is not central, not on our lips, not the ultimate point, then we are not engaging in New Testament missions work.

Good works will accompany the proclamation of Jesus, but they cannot replace it.

JESUS IS THE GAME CHANGER

Modern Christians get uncomfortable with the idea of gospel proclamation and the spread of the global church as the ultimate outcome of missions work for a few main reasons.

The first is a growing Western cynicism toward the church. I think many people, Christians included, have become disillusioned with the idea of church in general. Pick your poison: too traditional, too institutional, too political, poor leadership, personality driven, too wealthy, too corporate, too inward focused. Add your answer. Some of these criticisms might even be valid, even if a blanket application is unfair. But regardless of the underlying cause, there are a lot of cynics seeding doubt about the modern church's benefit to Western society. If we question it here, why would we want to replicate it in other parts of the world?

But the church, broken and imperfect, is God's idea not man's. It has been His mechanism for spreading the gospel and expanding His kingdom to a broken and imperfect world. We have 2,000-plus years to prove it. Newbigin sums it up quite clearly: "The mission of the Church is missions; the mission of missions is the Church."

Another reason we struggle to put Jesus and church expansion at the center of our missions efforts is that even God's people have an obsession with being liked. It's a "how many thumbs-up and hearts can I get" world out there nowadays. I know because I'm engaged in it, too. As I'm writing this book, I'm wondering how many people are going to like it. It's a normal human emotion. Addressing social ills and championing philanthropic endeavors garner universal praise. Who doesn't rally around anti-sex trafficking efforts and clean water? Adding the proclamation of Jesus to the mix just stirs up controversy and narrows our platform.

To make things worse, gospel proclamation is caricaturized by the obnoxious bullhorn preacher standing on top of his soap box on a downtown street corner yelling at the world they're going to hell. Who wants to be *that* guy? It's easier to just focus on "doing good" and keep Jesus out of it. And in that, I fear, we miss the whole point of the Great Commission.

Just to be clear, in case this needs clarification...

When we see the hungry, we feed them.

When we see the naked, we clothe them.

When we see the uneducated, we teach them.

When we see the marginalized and abused, we fight for them.

This has been the Spirit-led instinct of Christ followers for two thousand years. We bring the Kingdom wherever we go. But to everyone, at all times, and in all ways, we must proclaim the deity of Jesus, His life, death, and resurrection as the only hope for this sin-broken world. With our mouths. Making disciples of all cultures and nations is not yelling at them about how they're wrong and we're right. Making disciples of all cultures and nations is relationally showing them that we are all wrong, but there is a new Kingdom where Jesus is making all things right.

WHAT MISSIONS IS NOT

I attended a recent missions fundraiser where the well-meaning benefactor misquoted Jesus, fundamentally altering what He actually said. She noted with an excited sense of discovery, "And you know, after all, that the last thing Jesus told us before He ascended into heaven was to go into the whole world and represent Him, right?"

Wrong.

That sounds noble, representing Jesus and all, but it isn't the Great Commission. Although we are all called to be Spirit-empowered models of Jesus to the world around us, the Great Commission isn't about being nice and helping people solve problems. To review, here is the real command Jesus gave us from multiple Gospel accounts:

> *"Therefore, go and make disciples of all nations."*
> *(Matthew 28:19 NLT)*

"Go into all the world and preach the Good News to everyone." (Mark 16:15 NLT)

"[This] message would be proclaimed in the authority of his name to all the nations." (Luke 24:47 NLT)

Preach.

Proclaim.

Make disciples of all nations.

These words draw a line in the sand. They are truth claims, a call to repent and surrender, to die to self so we can have real life in Jesus. While the gospel is truly good news, it often isn't heard that way initially. Preaching and proclaiming won't always be welcomed, understood, or celebrated by the world around us, not in the way humanitarian efforts are embraced. And yet, this is the commission of our Savior. If it's not leading toward the proclamation of Jesus and the establishment of His church (making disciples) among all nations, it's not really missions.

How is your everyday work fulfilling the Great Commission? Has it impacted what you do with your earnings? Has it changed the way you pray? Is the gospel truly in your heart and on your lips? The marketplace is the perfect avenue for the demonstration and proclamation of the gospel.

Jesus wants to resurrect every people group on earth, and He's called each of us, great or small, employed by a church or working in the marketplace, to be the tellers of His Great Story.

– *Degrees for Missions* –

One of my greatest honors is serving on the Board of Regents at North Central University (NCU) in Minneapolis. Located in the heart of downtown Minneapolis, NCU is an exception to the rule when it comes to small Christian universities. They continue to reinvent themselves in strategic Kingdom ways, with business as mission as one of those ways.

Dr. William Tibbets is the Dean of the College of Business and Technology. He's also a longtime friend and former co-worker. When Bill transitioned out of church ministry, he took a teaching position in the business department at North Central, eventually becoming the dean, and was responsible for leading the resurrection of the business and technology program. Bill was one of the core reasons I gladly enrolled my daughter at NCU.

Once a school solely focused on training traditional pastors and missionaries, now NCU deploys their missional education through an expanding number of strategic marketplace degree programs as well. Bill and his colleagues in the College of Business and Technology (COBAT) don't just teach their students about business models, financial statements, and marketing techniques, they help them understand and embrace their sacred calling as followers of Jesus Christ. They release marketplace missionaries to water the earth with the gospel of Jesus Christ in their own communities and around the world.

We need more Christian institutions that embrace the sacred role of the marketplace in the demonstration and proclamation of the gospel around the world. I'm grateful for schools like North Central University that understand missionaries come in marketplace packages, too.

CHAPTER

15

BAM! Business as Mission

*When we add tangible value to society
through legitimate business, employing
locals, paying taxes, providing services,
physically improving our natural
surroundings, and integrating into [the
culture], it empowers a church-based identity.*

DICK BROGDEN

O ne of my greatest frustrations in recent years has been
the inability to openly share so many of the business as
mission stories I've encountered around the world. Due to the
sensitivity of almost every area where these stories happen, we
must disguise specific names and locations and whitewash most
details when we share in public arenas. It's a hard urge to resist in
today's social media culture.

But some of these stories must be told, and I will do my best to discretely share some of the ways the Great Commission is being fulfilled through business as mission around the world.

ENGLISH AS MISSION

On an island in East Africa, a business English school is planting the church among the unreached. I first visited this school in 2014 on one of my first overseas trips as the president of The Stone Table. The island is 99.9 percent Islamic, and while some mainlanders have started a Christian church for the expats who live there, there is no local, indigenous church. By definition, this people group, this *ethnos*, is completely unreached with the gospel.

Traditional missions methodologies won't work on this island. The country doesn't offer missionary visas. There is no Bible school in need of missionary teachers. There is hostility between neighboring countries that make "near-culture" missions work difficult and mostly untried, even by the local expat believers.

What this island nation does have is tourists. Lots of them. From Africa, the Middle East, Europe, and even the United States. The common language shared by nearly all tourists is English, and by learning "business English" (language training specifically focused on business settings) a local person can open up incredible new employment and socio-economic opportunities.

Our missionary friends recognized and seized this Kingdom opportunity in the marketplace. They launched a business English school and are planting the church through the business. The school meets a tangible need in the local community, but where many missions efforts embrace a compassion ministry, this business English school tackles an economic need. By providing a highly desired skill to the people of the island, they foster trust and relationships which gives them a platform for physical presence and ultimately gospel proclamation.

This is the beauty of business as mission. By meeting a real market need and hiring locals to work in the business, the missionaries become a true value-add to the local community. The marketplace is a perfect avenue for this kind of Kingdom demonstration and proclamation.

BANDA TIME

I experienced this firsthand during one of my visits to the island. The school structure includes both classroom and hands-on learning. At the end of each classroom session, the students gather in circles in the courtyard to practice their developing English skills with the teachers and missionary team members. They call it "banda time," named for the large gazebo structure they meet under outside the school. Banda time is vital for their learning and also provides a natural opportunity for building friendships and talking about spiritual matters.

I was placed in a circle with a half-dozen students and given a topic to foster dialog. That week's discussion centered on the word sacrifice. We discussed sacrificing something we wanted to buy now to save money for something more important later.

We talked about sacrificing our favorite dessert to lose weight and get healthier. Then the conversation turned more serious. The previous month, two young boys were caught stealing from the main market on the island. Even in the twenty-first century, punishment for these types of crimes can be severe in some Muslim cultures. Each boy had a hand cut off in a very public ceremony. The shock-and-awe penalty for this impropriety accomplished its desired effect as everyone on the island knew every gory detail.

"What if one of those boys was your son?" the teacher asked. "Would you have sacrificed your hand to save his? Would you have considered taking the punishment in his place?"

The group fell silent. I could see the students, some mothers themselves, processing the question through the lens of their own family and worldview.

After a long pause, one woman adamantly spoke up with her newly learned English language skills. "No! I would not take the punishment for him. Everyone must pay for their own sins."

"What if I told you that someone already paid the penalty for your sins?" the teacher asked, and the dialog quickly flowed into deep, gospel-saturated waters.

Unlike Western cultures, people in Muslim cultures are already having spiritual conversations. In fact, they welcome them! They expect Americans to be Christians, so they are not surprised or offended by talk of Jesus. Faith is not private in Islamic nations, and so these banda conversations naturally flow into coffee conversations and living room conversations and Bible conversations.

Through a small business that meets a market need, employs locals, and adds economic value to the community, the gospel is being demonstrated and proclaimed to a completely unreached people group. This is just one example of the power of the marketplace to engage the mission of God in the world.

"Through a small business...the gospel is being demonstrated and proclaimed to a completely unreached people group."

A MOMENT I WILL NEVER FORGET

During my most recent visit to the island, the missionaries reviewed our itinerary for the week. They had circled Saturday night as a special surprise—and was it ever.

A few months earlier, the school hired a guy named Charlie as a translator. Through his consistent interaction with the missionary-teachers, Charlie gave his life to Jesus. While Muslims are very open and interested in talking about Jesus, converting to Christianity is an abomination. Because of his decision to leave Islam, his wife's family revoked her marriage to Charlie. They had given her to Charlie as a Muslim man, but as a Christian man they were no longer obligated to honor the union, even though she wanted to remain his wife and was pregnant with their first child. Charlie's brothers threatened to kill him. They locked him out of his home and took all his possessions. Charlie was literally left alone with only the clothes on his back. Yet even amidst the most horrific persecution you could imagine, he refused to renounce his faith and allegiance to his Savior Jesus.

That Saturday night, I walked with Charlie and a small group of missionary English teachers to a small inlet of the Indian Ocean and witnessed the pastor of the tiny indigenous church baptize its newest member. This was the equivalent of seeing a stadium full of people respond to the gospel in other parts of the world, and all because a group of missionaries embraced the *marketplace* as part of God's Great Commission plan for the world.

WHAT IS BUSINESS AS MISSION?

In 2015, a 91-year-old Tom Paino visited me in my office. My childhood pastor and one of our founding board members was still larger than life to me. After handling all of our missions strategy and giving for over two decades, he knew it was time to pass the mantle. He was officially giving it to me, but it came with a specific request. Pastor Tom wanted me to drive to Springfield, Missouri to meet with the leadership of Assemblies of God World Missions (AGWM), our key global missions partner since our organization's inception. "Ask them what God is doing in the world right now and how your efforts in the coming years can best help move it forward," he instructed.

It felt like a divine moment.

For years, we had focused our missions efforts on pastoral training, usually through the tangible construction of Bible schools for the global church. While we are proud of what we were able to accomplish for that season, it seemed the Lord wanted to refocus our efforts for a new season of global missions impact.

My brother-in-law David and I hopped on I-70 out of Indianapolis and headed west. We met with AGWM Executive Director Greg Mundis for two hours and were blown away by what he confirmed in us. "Business as mission *must* become a key focus in the coming decades if we are going to fulfill the Great Commission," Greg shared. "I think you're uniquely positioned to help us champion this new movement."

This resonated deeply with what we were already feeling. Our core business model, CRF Affordable Housing, is a missional business in its own right. Our team works hard each day to demonstrate and proclaim the kingdom of God through adding value to the affordable housing market in our own community. To engage a global missions movement so in line with our own business as mission DNA just made sense, and it's a huge part of what we've been trying to do ever since.

THE BAM OFFICE

Our friends at AGWM believe in this direction so much that they spun-off a business as mission (BAM) entity (discoverbam.com) equipped with legal, financial, and strategic business talents, specifically aimed at supporting and sustaining this marketplace as missions movement. The Stone Table has come alongside the BAM office with a bullhorn and a backhoe, seeking to tell the story and build BAM engagement in the church and Christian business communities.

I love how the BAM office defines business as mission: "Business as mission is the intentional integration of business and ministry to create a sustainable, missional presence of the kingdom of God in a particular community."

- **Intentional Integration:** The ministry doesn't exist without the business, but the business cannot exist without its ministry intent.
- **Sustainable Presence:** The objective is to create real businesses that can economically support themselves for generations to come.
- **Missional Presence:** The marketplace provides the perfect mechanism to demonstrate the transformational power of the gospel and to proclaim the lordship of Jesus in communities around the world.

These core tenets can be seen so clearly through the business English school on that small Muslim island, but they're also manifesting around the world in many other contexts and forms. There is a trio of socioeconomic terms that BAM missionaries have adopted to help define their approach to business as mission work: job fakers, job takers, and job makers.

JOB FAKERS

This approach is somewhat self-explanatory and is part of the reason some BAM efforts have been criticized over the years. In this scenario, a missionary uses a fake business to gain entry into a foreign country. The business itself is just a shell and the missionary has no intent of adding value to the local marketplace in any way. The sign over the door is for access only, not for commerce.

These situations are troublesome mainly because they're inherently deceitful. If you want to proclaim the good news of Jesus, you should probably start by demonstrating a commitment to honesty and integrity. For that reason alone, job faking is a horrible approach to BAM work.

JOB TAKERS

Job takers do just that. They take a job with an existing company. With globalization in many sectors of the world economy, these opportunities are plentiful, including in and among many unreached people groups. Missionally-minded Christians are embedded in all kinds of global corporations in many UPG countries and communities. Missions movements like Scatter Global (scatterglobal.com) are intentionally equipping and connecting these job takers to proclaim the gospel and plant the church in places that missionaries traditionally cannot go.

Mobilizing job-taker missionaries is a powerful strategy paying huge Great Commission dividends around the world. Some drawbacks to job taking are the long work hours or complex work schedules these jobs may require; a lack of synergy and support in proclamation efforts; sudden job loss or salary reduction due to global economic downturns or pandemics; and the separation of expat housing from the local community that may come with certain jobs. Nevertheless, job taking has become a strategic BAM strategy for reaching the inconveniently lost.

JOB MAKERS

The most flexible and impactful (although admittedly the most risky and expensive) BAM model focuses on job making. These are the entrepreneurial endeavors. Job making identifies a market need in a strategic area, builds a business model to meet that need, employs locals to help run the operations of the business, and adds unique and authentic value to the local community.

The benefits of this BAM approach are plentiful. Not only does the missionary team have much more flexibility over their own schedules, but they are viewed as true value-add partners to the local economy. Business is a beautiful mechanism for serving others and for fostering relationships that allow the gospel to be demonstrated and proclaimed in these unreached areas.

MARKETPLACE SKILLS ARE MISSIONAL SKILLS

In an interview with my missionary friend Dick Brogden for The Stone Table website, I asked this real-life BAM practitioner why business has become such a vital mechanism for missions work.

Business goes beyond pragmatism. The pragmatic view is we can't get into these countries or access these communities unless we have a credible platform. That's true and legitimate. We do business, and we do it well, so that we can get visas and get into communities.

But it goes beyond pragmatism to fruitfulness. The normal person, if he had no job and no business, he might share the gospel with his neighbor, or the guy he buys fruit from, or his landlord, but he's not actually built to generate new relationships all day long so that he can keep sharing the gospel and see more people get saved.

Most people can't just generate new relational contacts out of thin air. They need a gym, they need a coffee house, they need a language center, they need a tourist company, they need a consulting corporation. They need something that propels them into life-on-life, face-to-face conversation with people.

You can't just sit in a coffee shop all day and think people are going to drop into your lap and say, "What must I do to be saved?" You need that credible offering to get out in community that is renewable. That renewable content is really important. Why? Because so many people hear the gospel and reject it.

If you don't have a way to meet new people, you're not going to see a lot of people saved. That's why business is not just pragmatic, but it's powerful, because it's continually

> *propelling us into new conversations, relationships, and opportunities where we can proclaim Christ, find those who are interested, and then drill down into discipleship with them.*[22]

Maybe this resonates with you. Perhaps one of these examples of how BAM creates access, adds real economic value, and fulfills the Great Commission around the world stirs something inside you. If you have marketplace skills, if you're an entrepreneur, you may have been unintentionally indoctrinated to believe your money is the only gift you have to offer the Kingdom. Don't get me wrong because financial generosity is vital! But the way God made you and wired you, the skillsets you developed in college or over the course of your career, all of it is designed to play a role in God's kingdom work in the world.

Is God calling you to invest in BAM development? Is God calling you to take your marketplace skills into a cross-cultural, unreached corner of the world for the sake of the gospel? Maybe you have a scalable business model and could offer an expansion or franchise to BAM practitioners on the field.

The marketplace is part of God's redemptive plan for the world. BAM is fulfilling the Great Commission to the ends of the earth, but let's bring those "ends of the earth" a little closer to home.

---

22   "Dick Brogden of Live Dead Discusses Missions and Using Business as Missions." The Stone Table. https://www.thestonetable.org/video-dick-brogden-of-live-dead-discusses-missions-and-using-business-as-missions/ (accessed April 21, 2021).

– *Take-a-Job Missionaries* –

Mobilizing marketplace believers is key to finishing the Great Commission in our lifetime. Some may wring their hands at the negative aspects of economic globalization, but the opportunities it opens for missionary efforts around the world cannot be ignored.

While entrepreneurship has proven its missional impact, strategically taking a job in the global economy is also sending missionaries into unreached areas with great effectiveness. Scatter Global (scatterglobal.com) is one of the organizations harnessing this movement. Through Scatter Global, marketplace missionaries can find jobs in unreached places around the world. Teach primary school in Turkey. Work as an ICU nurse in Azerbaijan. Take an IT sales position in India. These are all examples of job opportunities you can apply for today through Scatter Global, jobs that will put you in close proximity with unreached people groups on a daily basis through your everyday work.

Scatter Global's extensive training programs help job-takers rethink their missiology, embrace their work as a missions opportunity, transition into a cross-cultural living environment, and proclaim Jesus more boldly. Once on the field, Scatter Global connects these marketplace missionaries with strategic missionary organizations nearby. Groups like Live Dead, Pioneer, and Cru are just a few of their key partners on the ground. These missionary teams provide vital community support and connections as well as accountability to the Great Commission work that job-takers are there to engage.

You don't have to start a business to engage in business as mission. Groups like Scatter Global are making it possible to take strategic jobs in the global economy and fulfill your missional call to go to the unreached places of the world.

CHAPTER

16

The Diaspora

Taking the gospel to the ends of the earth has never been simply about God's people going from here to there; it's also been about ministering to those who've come from there to here.

PATRICK J. O'BANNON

A t this point in our journey, perhaps you've been convinced that your work is sacred. Maybe you're finally able to see your day job, as glamorous or menial as it may seem, through a redemptive gospel lens. Maybe you now see the role of the marketplace in God's kingdom work in the world and are awakened to a new awareness for unreached people groups and how business can be used to reach them for Jesus. Maybe you're feeling a pull to mobilize what you always assumed were just "secular" skills into God's Great Commission mandate.

But in the midst of all these new revelations, you're silently shouting: "There's no way I'm moving to another country!"

I get it. Every Christian kid (myself included) was terrified that developing a passion for global missions would ultimately lead to a life sentence in a tribal hut in Sub-Saharan Africa. It's something worth wrestling with, as Dick Brogden loves to challenge: "Everyone is called to go. The question you should wrestle with is whether or not God is allowing you to stay."

THE WORLD NEXT DOOR

Whether you live in Beirut, Lebanon or Lebanon, Indiana, unreached people groups are closer than you think. According to the United Nations 2017 International Migration Report, fifty million immigrants were living in the United States. That's nineteen percent of the world's migrant population.[23]

Unfortunately, immigration has become a powder-keg subject in some circles. For Christians who know Jesus' call to make disciples of all nations, the emergence of these diaspora communities in and among our own is a powerful opportunity for the gospel.

Diaspora, often referencing the dispersion of Jewish people outside Israel, is a term that can be used for any people group who leave their homeland and scatter abroad among other nations. The

---

23   "International Migration Report 2017." United Nations Department of Economic and Social Affairs. http://www.un.org/en/development/desa/population/migration/ publications/migrationreport/docs/MigrationReport2017_Highlights.pdf (accessed April 21, 2021).

growing ease of global mobility has created diaspora communities of nearly every culture and nationality around the world. Some are likely in your own backyard.

Which is literally true for me. We live in Avon, Indiana, a conservative suburb on the far west side of Indianapolis. We are the definition of the heartland, the Midwest, where traditional suburban neighborhoods with basketball goals in every driveway backup to corn and soybean fields. Even though we're just twenty-five minutes from Indy's urban center, it's not unusual to get stuck behind a large farm combine driving to work during planting or harvesting season.

And yet my next-door neighbor and his wife are Hindus from Mumbai. Sam oversees the opening of new Speedway gas stations all over the United States and his wife Diya works for a health insurance company. They're so proud of their son who recently graduated from pharmacy school.

The young couple behind us are also Hindus who moved here from India. Sai works for Salesforce in downtown Indianapolis, and his beautiful wife Kiara just had a gorgeous baby boy with the thickest head of black hair you have ever seen.

Across the street from us is an older Pakistani couple. I've had a harder time connecting with them as he does not speak English well and she rarely comes out in public where we can interact with her. He does wave at me with a huge smile whenever I catch him outside the house.

In the warmer months, a family walks by our house every night after dinner in full Indian attire, including a tall turban for the man. We regularly exchange greetings, although their lack of language skills makes them somewhat shy.

We live in the textbook definition of the Midwest, yet my family is the only Caucasian family in six contiguous houses at the entrance to our neighborhood. We send and support missionaries all over the world (as we should and will continue to do), and yet the world has literally moved into our neighborhood, too.

ENGAGING THROUGH THE MARKETPLACE

We have beautiful opportunities to reach out to these diaspora communities through traditional ministry models and by just being good old-fashioned neighbors. But in the same way we utilize business to employ, serve, and add value on the overseas mission field, we can reach these "backyard UPGs" through the marketplace as well.

Years ago, we joined hands with Catholic Charities to help place Burmese refugees in one of our Indianapolis apartment communities. We've hired multiple Burmese residents who now work on our staff to better serve these people as they transition to a new culture.

The resident demographic at one of our original properties in Columbus, Ohio was eighty percent Somali immigrants. Somalia is one of the most dangerous countries in the world, a place nearly impossible for any missionaries to live or work, yet we had access to hundreds of beautiful Somali families every day as we served them through affordable housing.

Our friends at T&W Construction, our general contractors on multiple assisted living developments, hired a Moroccan believer as one of their on-site superintendents. Ali was a persecuted Christian whose incredible journey to faith in Jesus was powerfully told in his book *The Apostate*.[24] Even though Ali and his family were already believers when they came to the States, his ongoing relationships within the local Muslim community through his work in the marketplace are slowly producing gospel fruit.

My friend Kevin was kicked out of North Africa during a government purge of foreign missionaries. That didn't stop him from pursuing the Muslim people he was called to serve. Back on the ground in Indianapolis, he launched multiple businesses and marketplace ministries aimed at creating opportunities for the growing number of Muslim cab drivers who had immigrated to the city. At one point, Kevin even owned a few cabs of his own, adding real value to the lives of men who came here seeking a better life. In Kevin, these diaspora communities found an advocate, a job, a friend, and an introduction to Jesus.

We support BAM missionaries to unreached people groups working in and around Morocco, Somalia, and North Africa. We also have missionary efforts to unreached people groups

---

24   *The Apostate: A Muslim's Path to Salvation* by Ali Boualou is available on Amazon. com.

from Morocco, Somalia, and North Africa who now live right here in Indianapolis! This diaspora reality is changing the global missions landscape in ways we cannot ignore. The Great Commission has literally moved in next door.

"The Great Commission has literally moved in next door."

PLANTING THE GLOBAL CHURCH FROM YOUR OWN BACKYARD

How do you engage this emerging world next door as a marketplace Christian? Just like cross-cultural missions work, we must be careful not to think too short-term or transactional. As Lausanne noted in their November 2020 Global Analysis, "the reality is many unreached people groups living in the city, such as Hindus and Buddhists, need time and relationship to come to grips with the biblical concept of God, creation, and sin before they can completely understand the gospel."[25] Relationships are always the currency of the Kingdom, and that's why every believer's holistic understanding of the sacred nature of their work and the role of the marketplace within God's creative order continues to be such a vital opportunity for the gospel.

How can your business serve these growing diaspora communities? What value can you add to their lives through the framework of the

---

25   Charles Rijnhart. "The World's Least Reached Are on Our Streets." Lausanne Movement. https://lausanne.org/content/lga/2020-11/the-worlds-least-reached-are-on-our-streets (accessed April 21, 2021).

marketplace? Do you have employment opportunities for cross-cultural staff members? In the same way we see business foster renewable human connections on the global mission field, how can your everyday work and marketplace skills help you foster real value-added relationships with those who have immigrated here from other countries? And ultimately, how do those relationships foster gospel conversations and point people to Jesus?

If you're like me, the Kingdom multiplication opportunity that exists in your literal backyard might be surprising. Due to technology, most of these diaspora communities remain deeply connected to their families and home communities. By reaching these people with the gospel on our soil, we have an opportunity to see Jesus redeem and resurrect the nations through our own backyard.

You may never travel to North Africa, but by engaging in business with a North African who lives in your local community, by employing a North African immigrant who moved to your town, by delivering cookies to your North African neighbor the week before Christmas, you might be sowing a gospel seed that will bear fruit thousands of miles from where it was planted.

If God is calling you to cross-cultural missions work, you better drop everything and get your passport updated. But while God is still calling missionaries to the nations, He's also bringing the nations to us. Look around you, my friends, the Great Commission just might be right outside your sliding glass door.

– Cross-Cultural – Entrepreneurship

I first heard about Sinapis, the Latin word for *mustard seed*, at a global missions meeting in Dubai. My dear friends from OneHope were hosting a global gathering of apostolic leaders to discuss cultural trends that the church needs to engage and empower.

At this particular meeting, we were talking about business and its role in the mission of God in the world. We were presented with various ministries and organizations that were already engaging this sphere well, and the work of Sinapis was held up as a best-in-practice model to consider. Strangely enough, Sinapis headquarters are located in Indianapolis, just ten miles from where I live. Since then, CEO Matthew Rohrs has become a friend and mutual encourager.

Sinapis engages indigenous entrepreneurs in eight strategic African countries. They work alongside the local church to equip and train entrepreneurs with key skills that will help them launch and sustain small- and medium-sized businesses in their own communities. All of Sinapis training is infused with gospel-centric materials, and Sinapis creates ongoing community to support these new business leaders in their work.

Sinapis believes local entrepreneurship is key to alleviating poverty and raising the quality of life in these African communities. In doing this alongside the local church, they synergize the spiritual and economic vitality of these businesses for life-giving Kingdom impact.

Sinapis is an inspiration, leveraging the marketplace not just as a funding mechanism for missions, but embracing business itself as part of God's redemptive work in the world. To date, they have trained thousands of African entrepreneurs and raised tens of millions in start-up funds to make these new businesses a reality. Just like a mustard seed, these small businesses are spreading their branches across the African continent to create new life, both tangibly and spiritually.

CHAPTER

17

The Currency of
the Kingdom

Business, after all, is nothing more than a
bunch of human relationships.

LEE IACOCCA

When The Stone Table launched in 2015, God gave us a vision for a business as mission community—a place where like-minded marketplace believers, aspiring entrepreneurs, and BAM missionaries can come together, work together, encourage one another, learn from one another, and engage the world through the marketplace. It's a multiplication vision that includes office space, a center for faith and work, an entrepreneurial incubator and accelerator, alongside co-working, retail, and gathering space for the community.

It's a mouthful and way bigger than me, but I saw a similar community named Moniker in Southern California and always felt a divine urge to bring something like it to the Midwest. Marketplace Christians are longing for relationships, discipleship, and encouragement. They want their work to matter to the Kingdom, but so many just don't know how.

I started searching for a building we could buy and transform. I drove all over greater Indianapolis, researched with brokers, and searched the online listings, but I couldn't find anything that checked all the boxes. Then one day I drove down Main Street in Speedway, Indiana.

FOLLOWING GOD'S LEAD

In the shadow of the world-famous Indianapolis Motor Speedway stands the old Allison Machine Shop, an 80,000-square foot historic warehouse built in the early twentieth century as an effort to improve race car engines. During WWII, it was converted to a manufacturing facility for airplane parts before finally re-emerging as a hub of Allison's robust manufacturing business in the decades that followed. It ceased operations in the 1980s, and from the outside, it appears to sit lifeless in the center of this quaint, small-town, throwback thoroughfare as a monument to its glorious past.

The sheer size and historical significance of the building made it incredibly attractive. With the rest of Main Street slowly coming back to life, why was its central anchor still sitting empty with its gorgeous storefront window openings all bricked up? I had to find out. I called an old church friend who sat on the town council and he shared the whole incredible story.

In the early 2000s, the machine shop was purchased by a wealthy land speculator from Florida (we'll call him Frank). Back in the '60s and '70s, Frank had been very successful buying and selling land in central Florida, just as the Walt Disney World craze was beginning to drive up property values. While Frank's methods were rumored as questionable, his success most certainly was not. He made *millions,* money he quickly began investing in his new obsession.

Ferraris.

To this day, Frank boasts one of the largest private Ferrari collections in the world, second only to an Arab sheikh from the Middle East. I've heard value estimates that range anywhere from $50 million to $100 million for the lot. His crown jewel is the oldest Ferrari still in existence, number three off the original assembly line. Even though the guts of the car have been removed, the shell alone is nearly priceless.

It turns out that Frank bought the old Allison Machine shop to function as a garage for his flashy car collection. How could I possibly convince a guy like Frank to sell me his Ferrari temple for our marketplace ministry campus?

When I first learned about Frank, he was serving a few years in a low-security prison in the Florida Panhandle. (He had gotten upside down with the IRS on some tax shelters, and the IRS won the argument.) My friend and I contemplated hopping on a plane to go visit him, but after an initial conversation with his son, we decided it might be best to wait until his "vacation" (as Frank liked to call it) was officially over.

A few weeks after his release, I found myself in line for an early morning Southwest Airlines flight from Indy to Orlando. Amidst giggling families in Bermuda shorts and Mickey Mouse T-shirts hopping on shuttles to the happiest place on earth, my buddy and I grabbed an Uber and headed for a much less magical place: a back corner booth at Denny's just three miles from Orlando International Airport.

I had dreams of pitching Frank a vision so compelling and saturated by the Holy Spirit that he would just load up his cars on flatbeds, find a new storage facility, and hand me the keys to our God-sized dream. God's plan was much different (and much longer). God's plan wasn't a building. God's plan was a friendship.

THE LONG VIEW

Over the next three years, Frank would fly into Indy to tend to his Ferrari collection or take in one of the multiple races hosted at the Indianapolis Motor Speedway. We often met up for lunch or dinner at his favorite Speedway restaurant where everyone literally knew his name. I would talk to him about business and missions, and he would talk about whisky and fast cars. We were an odd couple at best.

I unapologetically pitched him my faith-infused ideas for his building over countless Indiana tenderloins and he always seemed to listen. Frank had a vision of his own for that space: a museum to show off his exotic cars. If his museum never came to life, he said he would certainly consider selling the building to us. I was exuberant! Surely this was God's plan unfolding. I just needed to be patient and keep praying.

I had some version of this same conversation with Frank every time we met. In the spring he would tell me, "Maybe I'll be ready to sell it in the fall." In the fall he would tell me, "Maybe I'll be ready to sell it in the spring." As the months and years continued to tick by, I found myself struggling to keep the faith.

Then one day Frank informed me that he had cancer. The prognosis was encouraging, but the sobering news opened up conversations of mortality and eternity. Over another of our semi-regular lunches, the dialog turned to Jesus. I would like to tell you Frank was soft and open and allowed me to pray with him that day. The reality was quite the opposite. Frank grew up as an Episcopalian and was even an altar boy in his church until his late teens. It was in that season Frank claims he finally realized that God was a farce, that this world was all there is, and that he was going to suck the marrow out of the years he had on earth.

I tried to share the truth of the gospel with him as best I could, to tell him there was a much bigger story, that there really is a Savior, and that the anemic religion he experienced as a child was not who Jesus really is. When I asked if I could pray for him, he said "You can do whatever you want, but I don't believe in any of that fairytale [expletive]."

SOMETHING GREATER THAN A BUSINESS TRANSACTION

As we left the restaurant, we stood on the front step and looked at Frank's building. Once again, he gave me the same line, "Maybe I'll be ready to sell it next spring."

I went back to my car depressed and sat for a few minutes with the engine off. "Lord, what is this all about? I don't seem to be making any inroads toward securing the building. To make things worse, Frank completely rejected You. I feel like I've taken this vision You gave me and put it all in the hands of a pagan man. I'm waiting for *him* to give *Your* plans permission to go forward. What is going on here?"

I don't claim to hear audible voices, but in that honest moment in a parked car on Main Street in Speedway, Indiana, I felt the Holy Spirit clearly say, "It's okay to move on now."

That afternoon, I put Frank and his building in God's hands and began to ask what His new plan might be. Less than forty-eight hours later, I got a call from a friend who felt compelled to reach out to me. He couldn't stop thinking about The Stone Table campus concept I had shared with him about a year earlier and wondered if I had ever considered a different part of the city to bring the concept to life. I told him that I had not but promised that I would pray about it.

Six months later, we purchased a prime piece of property out of foreclosure for pennies on the dollar in one of the fastest growing areas of Indianapolis. We are currently working on plans to bring God's vision to life there.

WHAT WAS GOD UP TO ANYWAY?

"Business transactions foster relationships, and relationships are the currency of God's kingdom."

Is it possible that the passion God put in my heart for Frank's building actually had little or nothing to do with the building at all and everything to do with Frank himself? Did God, in His infinite patience, want to reach out just one more time to this hard-hearted man with the grace and mercy of Jesus? I think He did. In fact, I'm sure He did.

That real estate transaction may have gone cold, but it was the pursuit of a business deal that put me in proximity with a man who desperately needed Jesus. While that story doesn't have a happy ending (at least not yet!), it is the perfect example of why the marketplace must be reimagined and re-embraced as part of God's Great Commission game plan.

Business transactions foster relationships, and relationships are the currency of God's kingdom. Whether in our own communities or in the far reaches of the world, the marketplace is the perfect channel for the love and grace of Jesus to be demonstrated and proclaimed!

In this moment, please stop and say a short prayer for Frank's heart to soften to Jesus. That's not his real name, but God will know who you're talking about.

– *Marketplace Community* –

I was sitting in a world-famous dessert restaurant in the Gaslamp Quarter of downtown San Diego texting an old friend when I realized we were just a few blocks from each other. I was there for a conference and on a whim decided to reach out to him as I knew he was from the area. We had met rather serendipitously a few years earlier when he visited the church I was pastoring in Indianapolis, and we had stayed in touch via social media.

"You're just a few blocks from me," he messaged back. "When you're done sugaring yourself up, come down here and see what we're up to."

Sugar in my system, we strolled up the balmy San Diego streets until we came to an old warehouse buzzing with activity. Dozens of twenty-somethings were hauling all kinds of trash and construction debris to a couple of large dumpsters at the loading dock.

"Welcome to Moniker Warehouse!" My friend Ryan is a burgeoning entrepreneur with a passion for connecting people. While holding down an 8-5 with a high-end marketing company, he spent his off-hours working a deal on a piece of downtown real estate with some friends. Their vision was to create a space that would bring entrepreneurs and marketplace dreamers together in community.

They call it a "dream factory," and today it boasts dozens of start-ups and small businesses working from the same creative space together. This is not just a place to rent an office; it's a place to find synergy and human connection. Over the years, Moniker Warehouse has expanded to become five different retail, office, co-working, and event spaces around the greater San Diego area.

While the principles in this endeavor are believers in Jesus, they don't call it a "Christian business" per se. They draw people in with the contagion of community, support, and connection, and from there the gospel comes to life in and through their lives.

The Moniker vision is so enticing that we hope to model many of its components in our own marketplace campus here in Indianapolis. The gospel is just waiting to be demonstrated and proclaimed through marketplace community.

18

Sharing Jesus in the Marketplace

Proclaiming the gospel to a lost world
cannot be just another activity to add to the
church's crowded agenda. It must be central
to who we are. It forms our identity.

FRANCIS CHAN

My daughter is a freshman at Indiana University in Bloomington, Indiana. The 200-year-old school is tucked into the rolling hills of southern Indiana and boasts a beautiful web of tree-lined walkways connecting the 1,933-acre historic campus. Whether you're a student or not, it's an absolutely lovely place to take an afternoon stroll.

The transition from high school to college is full of new experiences, and Anna regularly texts her mom and me about things she encounters while walking to class, the student union, or her dorm. One day early in the spring, my phone buzzed with a perplexed message.

An angry woman with a wooden cross was standing next to a bunch of homemade posterboard signs about Jesus and yelling at Anna and the other passing students. She told my daughter her clothes were inappropriate and then called her a derogatory name. She shouted similar things at all the other girls. Apparently, this woman and her husband make this a regular practice on college campuses across the country. They call it "confrontational evangelism," but this kind of intentionally combative distortion of biblical proclamation leaves students ridiculing more than repenting.

Most genuine Christians don't want to be associated with this kind of abrasive, guerilla-style assault masquerading as a proclamation tactic. It's this arrogant (proud of being more bold than brokenhearted in love for the lost), confrontational approach to sharing our faith that has caricaturized Christians as angry bullhorn proselytizers.

Maybe you know a guy like this in your office. He probably doesn't use a bullhorn (if he does, please send a video), but his tactics for sharing about Christ with co-workers are aggressive, prideful, and relationally alienating at best. None of us want to be that guy. Depending on where you work, human resources may not let you be that guy. But it begs the question: How do I share my faith in the marketplace without being weird?

To be clear, gospel proclamation isn't always warm and fuzzy. Sometimes a prophetic voice will feel abrasive and odd, especially to our modern Western mindset. The gospel confronts us with bad news before it becomes the good news, and if we're honest, the Bible is filled with somewhat weird guys preaching the gospel. The gospel is offensive to our sin-worn humanity, but how do we make sure it's the gospel that's actually doing the offending? In a sense, how do we embrace the *right kind* of weird?

> "The Bible is filled with somewhat weird guys preaching the gospel."

I don't know if I do this well, but I want to do it better. As we discussed more fully in previous chapters, there is no missions without proclamation. But when I see how relational, intentional, and natural so many of our BAM missionaries make gospel proclamation in their overseas context, I wonder why we don't bring that same missionary mindset into our own marketplace encounters. We don't want to sell Jesus like a pushy telemarketer, but we've already seen what a natural conduit the marketplace creates for the gospel. How can we better embrace it? The first and most important step is making sure the gospel has truly captured you.

IS THE GOSPEL REAL TO YOU?

I grew up in church. I was a leader in the youth group. I wore Christian T-shirts to school, carried my Bible, supported all the on-campus student ministries. I ultimately became a music pastor and wrote dozens of songs to help the church worship God. I planted a church and have preached hundreds of sermons. Now, we run a business that was founded to support the global proclamation of Jesus. I don't remember a day that my intellectual faith in Christ has ever waivered.

While I have been a devout believer during every season of my life, the gospel has become much more real to me the older I have gotten. Not because I'm more pious or intelligent now, but because I've simply lived long enough to realize how incapable I am of fixing myself.

Younger Christian Erik "sold" Jesus as a moralistic self-help method.

Older Christian Erik gushes Jesus as life-sustaining oxygen for a drowning man.

Without Jesus, I'm not bad. Without Jesus, I'm dead. This distinction changes everything.

For many believers, sharing their faith is more akin to getting a friend to sign-up for their multi-level marketing business. But when the gospel has truly come alive inside of you, it flows forth like streams of living water bearing fruit in good season (Psalm 1).

THE WORKPLACE BISHOP

I've known my friend Darren and his wife Cathy for over thirty years. For most of that time, Darren worked in full-time vocational ministry, first as a teacher in a Christian school, then as the children's pastor for two mega-churches here in the greater Indianapolis area.

Darren and I somewhat serendipitously ran into each other at a local restaurant a few months back where he began to share with me his unusual ministry career path. A lot of Christians I know start out working in the marketplace, begin volunteering at their church, and then ultimately end up on the church staff. That was my path to pastoral ministry. Darren sort of reverse-engineered that strategy.

After three decades in what some would consider the pinnacle of vocational ministry, Darren felt led to step away. In the interim, he picked up a few part-time jobs to pay the bills. He drove for Uber, worked as a courier, and ultimately ended up at a large logistics shipping company loading and unloading the airplanes.

Darren's friends were perplexed. "What happened, man? What did you do? Why did you lose your ministry?" Those were the typical assumptions. Whenever someone moves from vocational ministry back into the marketplace, especially into a role like Darren's, it's usually due to the fallout of some scandal. But it was in this seemingly backward move that Darren discovered a whole new ministry.

Parking airplanes and unloading boxes wasn't what Darren aspired to in his post-church career. In fact, he had been preparing his resume to go looking for a new church gig. Then one night, he had a dream. He saw himself in a large stadium wearing a fancy suit preparing to preach a sermon. The musicians were finishing up a powerful time of worship and the seats were packed to the rafters. Darren had his sermon notes all prepared, but just as he was about to step up to the podium to start preaching, the lights went out. It was pitch black. He shouted to the massive congregation, encouraging them to hold tight until the power could be restored. But when the lights came back up, everyone was gone. The entire stadium was empty, except for twelve lonely people. They were looking around at the empty seats wondering why everyone was gone. It seemed awkward to preach to just twelve people from the stage, so Darren asked them to move to the front and sit on the floor. He came down and joined them in a circle. Then he woke up.

Darren hadn't thought much about the dream until he was sitting in the breakroom at his logistics job one day. He had fallen in love with his "secular" work. The hours he spent with his rough and tumble co-workers actually breathed new life into him.

Through a conversation, they learned Darren was a former pastor. They dubbed him "preacher man" until one of his colleagues was up late watching TV one night and channel surfed past a message from T. D. Jakes. After that, Darren's official nickname became "The Bishop."

Darren never became a hardcore Jesus salesman, but he did begin to look for natural opportunities to share his faith with his co-workers. One guy shared about a frustrating relational situation with one of his kids, and Darren asked if he could pray for him. One lady had her arms tattooed with mystic symbols, and in asking what they meant Darren turned the conversation to his faith in Christ. The Bishop was being winsome with his witness.

As his ragtag team sat around the table in the lunchroom one day, Darren recalled the dream of that stadium blackout that turned tens of thousands of people into a dirty dozen. He shared the story with his new friends. One of the guys looked around the table and counted heads. There were twelve of them. "Hey, Bishop, I think that dream was about us."

Even after all those months, Darren never put it all together. What he thought was a temporary detour to make ends meet while he looked for a new ministry position actually became his ministry position.

NO BULLHORN NECESSARY

On April 15, 2021, a disgruntled former employee with known mental health issues walked into part of the shipping facility where Darren works at the Indianapolis International Airport. The young man opened fire, tragically killing eight staff members before turning the gun on himself. His victims ranged in age from 19 to 74. One of the young girls killed used to play basketball versus my daughter in high school. The news rocked our city and quickly became national news.

Darren knew the company's grief counselors would be overrun the next day, so he took up his informal title of Bishop and ran toward the aftermath, in his words, "like a fireman running into a burning building." He had many powerful conversations with co-workers who were confused, mourning, and terrified.

The following week, Darren's supervisors called a team meeting to discuss the tragedy and how to improve security at the hub. After the brainstorming session had carried on for some time, Darren spoke up and asked what kind of proactive measures the company was willing to take. "What if one of us had taken an interest in this young man, I mean really loved him and sought his best," he said. "Would this have ever happened?"

Darren told his managers that he sees his role in the organization as investing in and helping people as they work together to better the company. The managers were intrigued enough that they asked him to draft a proposal for a potential new role as a life coach and chaplain.

Being available, being genuinely concerned with both the work and the people who do it, opens incredible opportunities for the gospel. Darren's investment into workplace relationships gives him access into peoples' lives in ways that allow the proclamation of Jesus to naturally move forward. He doesn't need a bullhorn on the street corner because he's close enough physically and relationally that his co-workers hear every word he speaks.

A "BE RELATIONAL" HOW-TO

Relationships are the currency of any good business. They're also the currency of God's kingdom. This is a key overlap. All great relationships are rooted in mutual trust.

When CRF Affordable Housing first started developing new construction projects, I was taken back by how difficult it was to connect with the local municipalities in the communities where we were trying to build. There was a standoffishness, an uncomfortable relational distance. Developers didn't trust municipalities and municipalities didn't trust developers. This is true of general contractors and subcontractors as well. The development world is filled with relational dysfunction, which stems from decades of fraud, lies, empty promises, and political posturing on all sides of the equation. If the development business was a marriage, the parties would be in consistent and constant counseling.

On more than one occasion, I have had to look a councilmember or local town manager in the eye and passionately declare, "We are far from perfect. We will definitely make mistakes. But our company will never intentionally defraud or deceive you. If we tell you something, we mean it. You can count on us." I've even had to hold to some early commitments I made when I found out later we might have been able to avoid them. Simply caring about people, doing good work, owning your mistakes, and committing to the truth will differentiate you from others in such a dramatic way that people will wonder what's different about you. These simple, God-honoring, common sense strategies are not just good business practice; they will most certainly lead to opportunities to share your faith with others.

Let's get practical. How do you share Jesus in the marketplace without being weird?

Be real: If the gospel has not swallowed you up in all of its grace-filled glory, you'll be selling Jesus instead of sharing Jesus. Saturate yourself in the unmerited love of Christ, feel the full weight of your complete lostness apart from Jesus, experience the futility of all your self-salvation efforts, and the resurrection power of the gospel will explode from your life in ways that cannot be contained. Throw yourself more fully on Jesus and see what fruit starts to grow.

Be natural: Relationships are the currency of the Kingdom. Get to know people genuinely. Listen to their stories, their backgrounds, their joys, and their pains. Jesus flows naturally from life to life, and the marketplace creates ongoing, renewable relationships with those who need to hear the gospel. We're not selling a product like an unsolicited telemarketer; rather, we're sharing our lives—our resurrected lives—with those who desperately need the Source of our redemption.

Be intentional: While no one likes the aggressive, bullhorn Jesus salesman, we can't reject that caricature only to embrace the opposite fallacy that being real and natural means avoiding any discomfort at all. Sharing our faith with others doesn't have to be aggressive and offensive in its delivery, but the gospel does challenge our sin before it redeems us from it. Look for little moments, opportunities to pray for people in need, off-handed comments that might reveal an openness to spiritual conversations. Love isn't passive, and intentional doesn't have to be obnoxious.

I have a friend who asks every waiter how his family can pray for them as they prepare to bless the meal they just served. In hundreds of encounters, he's only had two people turn him down.

Many still mention the power of those prayers in their lives the next time he visits the restaurant.

In dealing with a vendor that completely botched their service to us, I was able to share one of my greatest leadership shortcomings with them on a conference call. While not letting them off the hook for their mistakes, I framed our next steps by confessing, "I need people to give me grace, and we're extending that same grace to you today as well. Now let's get to work."

It's these kinds of moments that open people to gospel conversations. It doesn't have to be weird. People are hungry for Jesus, even if they don't realize what that gaping hole is in their lives quite yet. Look for intentional moments for simple proclamation. Let the gospel be the gospel. Grace is contagious. You might be surprised what God will do through you.

– *Contagious Giving* –

Diane has been an incredibly successful custom home builder in the Bloomington, Indiana market for decades. Her love for Jesus and His kingdom has been a driving force in the way her company does business and the level of excellence she brings to her craft.

She and her husband have been long-time members of Cornerstone Christian Fellowship, the church my brother- and sister-in-law planted in 1996 on the south side of this famous college town. In much the same way as I was raised in church, one can't sit under David's pastoral leadership for long without developing a huge heart for global missions. It oozes from the pulpit in one way or another each Sunday and is reflected in the church's massive annual support of strategic missionaries and missions projects.

A few years ago, David shared a vision with his congregation for reaching China through a series of business as mission projects. The Stone Table was offering matching funds, doubling every dollar given by Cornerstone and other partner churches. Diane was deeply inspired, not only by the opportunity to proclaim Jesus among a key unreached people group in the area, but by the multiplication possibilities. Her entrepreneurial gene kicked in.

Diane called her friend Lisa, a local interior designer, and pitched a God-inspired idea. "Let's share this missions opportunity with a bunch of our industry colleagues and offer to match every dollar they give." So, they started sending emails, making calls, and scheduling lunches. A few short weeks later, Diane and Lisa had commitments for $50,000 and matched it with $50,000 of their own! If that wasn't incredible enough, these funds were matched *again* by The Stone Table! It was exponential multiplication.

Giving is contagious. Diane and Lisa could have quietly contributed to that strategic missions opportunity on their own and left it at that. But it's so much more fun to be generous with others. The Kingdom is we, not me.

As marketplace believers, we are called to steward the resources we've been given for this Great Commission mandate. All believers carry the responsibility of reaching the nations with the gospel. God blesses the hands of those who make His passion their own, and God's agenda is missions. Diane and Lisa are a beautiful model of contagious marketplace generosity.

19

Conclusion

*Most people plot and plan themselves into
mediocrity, while now and again somebody
forgets himself into greatness.*

E. STANLEY JONES

My greatest hope for this book is that it would help just one person reimagine their everyday work with gospel-resurrected meaning and purpose. Whether you're a high school science teacher or the CEO of a manufacturing company, your work is a sacred calling when you dedicate it to God. From our own communities to the ends of the earth, the marketplace was designed to be an ongoing part of God's kingdom mission in this world. The gospel truly redeems and resurrects all things, including the work of our hands.

We have looked at our work through the lens of the Great Story, the Great Commandment, and the Great Commission.

THE GREAT STORY

I dedicated this book to my father, a business as mission practitioner who never fully realized the God story he was stepping into. In fact, he's probably reading this now wondering what in the world he ever did that would be considered all that special (which is part of the reason why I think it is special). If we're going to find our story where it belongs in the Great Story of God, it's going to require a whole lot of forgetting about ourselves.

My dad spent the first thirty years of his career working, learning, investing, risking, and building. Heading into what could have been the most personally lucrative season of his entrepreneurial career, he re-routed those years to a nonprofit real estate start-up that would amass assets for the Kingdom instead of his personal balance sheet. I believe my dad answered his *vocare*, his calling.

My 21-year-old father once dreamed of having one million dollars in the bank. My 77-year-old father has made that one million dozens of times over—except none of it is in his own bank account. My dad is my hero, one of the richest men in the world by my math.

You don't have to give decades of your life to running a missions-based nonprofit for your work story to become part of God's Great Story. For-profit businesses and big personal balance sheets can be Kingdom assets, too! But you do have to surrender your self-appointed role as author of your own narrative.

What is the Holy Spirit saying to you? How can your everyday work, whatever it may be, find its full meaning and purpose within the Great Story of God?

THE GREAT COMMANDMENT

A few years ago, our housing company adopted an unofficial motto: We wash feet. It really stuck. I see it regularly on email taglines. I hear it in meeting discussions. I even see it in pictures and graphics hung around our offices. We're in the housing business; we're not podiatrists. We lease apartments; we don't give pedicures. What does this mean?

This imagery is an intentional nod to Jesus washing His disciples' feet, a story found in three of the four Gospel accounts. While not all of our eighty-plus employees are professing Christians, the concept still resonates. Leaders lead by serving people.

> *And since I, your Lord and Teacher, have washed your feet, you ought to wash each other's feet. I have given you an example to follow. Do as I have done to you. (John 13:14–15 NLT)*

This is true of all work. When the alarm goes off each morning, we have another opportunity to support ourselves and our families through serving and adding value to the lives of other human beings. We do this in big and small ways, in complicated and simple ways, in celebrated and anonymous ways. Good work of any kind is always about "washing feet."

As we discussed at length, our work is a daily opportunity to engage what Jesus said was most important: honoring God and loving our neighbor. This is true, not just of white-collar jobs in fancy office suites, but of assembly lines and restaurants, and of day laborers all over the world. We don't just honor God and love our neighbor by acts of charity; we honor God and love our neighbor by acts of commerce.

What is the Holy Spirit saying to you? How can your everyday work, whatever it may be, become that beautiful fulfillment of the Great Commandment?

THE GREAT COMMISSION

One of my greatest honors in recent years has been to serve on the Board of Regents at North Central University (NCU). As a long-time friend of the Dean of the College of Business and Technology, I was already familiar with the school and its surging business program. The business school has nearly quadrupled in students over the past few years as more and more young Christians seek to find their calling in the marketplace.

Originally known as North Central Bible College, NCU still has a large number of pastoral and missionary students preparing for more traditional ministry careers. But it's the way North Central is intentionally bringing these two paths together that has me the most energized.

At a recent Board of Regents meeting, NCU president Scott Hagan shared his ongoing conversations with the leadership of Assemblies of God World Missions that focused on the urgent need for marketplace believers in every sphere of life. "When I talk with our missionary leaders, they're telling me that we need teachers, that we need biologists and chemists, that we need marketers and entrepreneurs and businesspeople of all kinds, not just to create more Christians in these fields, but for very specific Great Commission strategy. We need them to become great at their craft and then disperse all over the world, taking their work skills and the gospel with them wherever they go."

"The marketplace is the future of global missions."

I believe the marketplace is the future of global missions, that business as mission is not just some trendy global missions fad, but a vital part of fulfilling the Great Commission in our lifetime. As the church reawakens to the sacred role of the marketplace, it will be redeemed not only to demonstrate the Kingdom of God but to proclaim the name of Jesus to the ends of the earth.

What is the Holy Spirit saying to you? How can your everyday work, whatever it may be, become that powerful fulfillment of the Great Commission?

CLOSING TIME

In the late 1990s, the American rock band Semisonic released their signature song, "Closing Time." The last line leaves you feeling somewhat pensive about the seasonal motion of this life: "Every new beginning comes from some other beginning's end."

That's where our housing company, CRF Affordable Housing, finds itself today.

I chipped away at this manuscript over a five-month span as my work schedule allowed. When I started writing, I never imagined we would be making some of the seismic shifts that are now officially underway.

Because of the collision of multiple economic factors, our board and leadership team decided to sell a major portion of our multifamily apartment portfolio and pivot into other affordable housing opportunities. In thirty years, we have only sold one property, so this is an overwhelming move for us. We have consistently said we are in this business to stay in this business. But the truth is, we only steward these assets, we do not own them. The pillar of God's presence seems to be clearly moving us in a new direction, and we are doing our best to obediently follow.

Even though the sale process will likely take six to nine months, we wanted to tell our on-site staff as quickly as possible. After a painful all-staff conference call, we jumped in the car for a three-day tour of each site to meet with our teams, look them in the eyes, listen to their questions and concerns, and do our best to let them know how much we love them.

We all shed tears over those three days.

"I don't want to work for anyone else," a manager lamented.

One maintenance supervisor joked, "I'm not going to enjoy fixing drywall if it's not helping someone in another country."

"This is the greatest company I've ever worked for," another shared. "I was planning to work here until I retired."

"I've talked about God more during my two years working here than I have my entire life."

"Thank you for your prayers! I believe those prayers have led us back to Jesus."

As we headed back to the home office, I thanked our operations director for helping us build a company and a culture so unique and God-honoring that people weep over it when a season comes to an end. We rarely get to see the whole picture, but occasionally God gives us a quick glimpse of what He can do when we submit the work of our hands to His Great Story, Great Commandment, and Great Commission.

"Did you ever imagine this kind of impact when you and the board launched this company thirty years ago?" I asked my dad. "Look what God has done through the simple, obedient work of your hands."

As we pivot into the next three decades with that same heart and spirit—to glorify God through our work and accelerate the Great Commission through the marketplace—I have no doubt He will continue to do it again and again.

And He will do it through you, too. Your marketplace work has a sacred role in God's kingdom work in the world. Surrender your story to God's Great Story, wake up every day with a renewed passion to honor God and add value to those around you through your work, and take every opportunity to proclaim the name of Jesus in your local community and to the ends of the earth.

This isn't just the calling of the "professional" Christians. It's time for marketplace believers to rise up and embrace their sacred Kingdom calling.

Worship God.

Love your neighbors.

Make disciples of every nation.

Not one aspect of the true Christian vocation has changed in two thousand years. No distractions. No sideways energy. Faithful worship. Faithful service. Make much of Jesus. Let's get to it.

ABOUT THE AUTHOR

After starting his career in the business world, Erik Cooper spent twelve years in full-time ministry, both on staff at a large suburban church and as a church planter in a downtown urban context, before returning to the marketplace. In addition to his role at The Stone Table (thestonetable.org), he serves as Vice President at Community Reinvestment Foundation (crf.net), a nonprofit real estate company that owns, manages, and constructs high-quality affordable housing and assisted living facilities while investing half its profits each year into global missions through The Stone Table. In his spare time, he enjoys playing the piano, playing mediocre golf, crafting quality dad jokes, and drinking entirely too much coffee. Erik and his wife Mandy reside in Indianpolis, Indiana with their three incredible children Emma, Anna, and Austin, who make their lives so rich.

🐦 erikcooper 📘 erikcooper 📷 erikcooper 💼 erikcooper74

thestonetable.org // crf.net // erikcooper.me

CPSIA information can be obtained
at www.ICGtesting.com
Printed in the USA
BVHW040405181021
619129BV00003B/15